C000181386

The Story of
TIMBERTROVE

Shirley O'Kelly

To ELENA

OAK·TREE·PRESS

Shirley O'Kelly

Published by Oak Tree Press, Cork, Ireland

www.SuccessStore.com

© 2022 Shirley O'Kelly

A catalogue record of this book is available from the British Library.

ISBN 978 1 78119 537 6

Cover photo: Ramsey Cardy

Cover design: Kieran O'Connor Design

Print: SprintPrint, Dublin

All rights reserved. No part of this publication may be reproduced or transmitted in any form or by any means, including photocopying, recording or electronically without written permission of the publisher. Such written permission also must be obtained before any part of this publication is stored in a retrieval system of any nature. Requests for permission should be directed to Oak Tree Press, info@oaktreepress.com.

CONTENTS

TIMBERTROVE

BETTER TIMES

INTRODUCTION

Henry and I would like to share a story with you.

It's a story of two young people, from ordinary backgrounds, who both left school early, mad keen to work, and who found they shared the same dreams of success.

It's a story of how we succeeded in achieving our dreams – through hard work, ongoing learning, a lot of help and a bit of luck.

It's a story of how we overcame two recessions – though the last one almost cost us everything – through sheer self-belief and determination.

It's a story of a small family business, with super, hard-working, loyal employees, that grew and retrenched – and grew again.

It's a story of the challenges of running a small business today – the day-in, day-out grind, the obstacles and hassles.

It's a story of the joy of running a small business today – meeting and serving customers, freedom in decision-making, seeing the direct results of your efforts.

It's a story – beginning again in the third-generation – of a family of entrepreneurs.

Most of all, it's our story – the story of Shirley and Henry, of O'Kelly's Sawmill and Timbertrove, of up and downs, good times and bad. It's the story of our dreams made real.

We hope you find our experiences interesting and that you learn something from them.

Shirley O'Kelly
Timbertrove
Dublin, August 2022

EARLY DAYS

MY CHILDHOOD

I came from a large family: six boys and five girls. We lived in a small, 969 sq. ft, three-bedroomed terraced house in a cul-de-sac in Churchtown: 18 Braemor Drive.

My parents, Ernie and Helen Callaghan, married in 1954. They only had one wage – £6 per week – coming into the house, as my mother had to leave her job in Jacobs when she got married. The company had a long-standing policy that no female member [of staff] could work once they got married. No "Women's Lib" back then!

A year later, their first son, Trevor, was born. He was followed by three daughters: Audrey, Susan and then me.

The Callaghan children (except Darell, the youngest) in 1969: (from left back)
Trevor, Audrey, Susan, Shirley, Elaine, Hilary, Stanley, Roger, Keith and Ian –
all in Aran jumpers knitted by Mum.

In 1958, Mum and Dad decided to set up their own business – Ernie Callaghan Motorcycles & Cycles – in a small workshop at the back of the house. As the family grew, the business needed to grow too, to support them all. So Ernie and Helen decided to set up a shop on Landscape Road in Churchtown.

Ernie, chatting to a customer outside his motorcycle shop.

Ernie and Helen were always on the go. Between working long hours in the shop, doing accounts, dealing with the bank, collecting parts between school runs, constantly washing, ironing, baking, cooking, sewing, knitting, they still found time to be on some mountain or race track every single solitary Saturday and Sunday, all 13 of us! To this day, I am still amazed as to how they managed!

Us children all had to take turns in working in the shop after school. We did our homework between stacking shelves and serving customers. And we did not get paid; it was just something we had to do to help! Despite not having much money, no new clothes or holidays, we had great times and it was a good upbringing.

I think this is how we became such a competitive family. As we grew up, we had to fight for everything. We were constantly competing!

HENRY'S CHILDHOOD

Henry is from a much smaller family. He has three younger brothers: Fintan, Padraig and Niall. His parents, Fintan and Joan, lived in Killakee, beside Lord Massy's estate.

The O'Kelly family: Fintan Senior, Niall, Padraig, Fintan, Joan and Henry.

Fintan operated as a sole trader, running a plant hire business. Joan ran a small farm and was also general manager in Killakee House, which at the time was an art gallery, boutique, giftshop and tearooms.

Henry also worked in Killakee House after school and during his summer holidays. His jobs ranged from helping to make sandwiches in the tearooms to serving tables. He also sold clothes in the boutique and recalls telling the women how well the clothes suited them and how lovely they looked. On opening nights of exhibitions at the art gallery, Henry would serve the wine. The guests would ask him if it was a sweet or dry wine; he hadn't a clue! He also had to clean the toilets and, of course, as the eldest son, he was on alarm call!

The only office work experience he did was on a Wednesday after school in Newspread, a magazine distributor. Instead, from a very young age, Henry worked outdoors on local farms cleaning sheds, feeding cows, making hay and doing other chores. He got the opportunity to drive tractors and machines on the farms and also drove loading shovels as his uncles were involved in gravel pits.

After working for two summers, Henry finally got his first payment from one of the local farmers: "a pair of brand new wellies"!

One of Henry's uncles cut turf up on the Featherbeds, which Henry would help with, but it was hard work cutting the turf, bringing it down to the side of the road and loading it onto the trailer by hand.

STARTING MY CAREER

When I was 15, with summer holidays coming up, I dreaded going back to school after completing my Junior Cert. All I wanted was to get out and earn decent money – not just pocket money, which then was nothing like what you would get now. I could not wait to be able to buy my own new clothes, eat out in a restaurant and go on a holiday. These were things I had yet to experience!

And then an opportunity came. A good friend of the family, Michael Orr, set up a new motor leasing business. He asked my Dad, Ernie, if one of his daughters wanted a summer job. Dad said, "Shirley will take the job".

This was my chance! I thought, "Right, all I need to do is make a good impression and I won't have to go back to school in September!" That was enough of an incentive for me to do whatever the job required; whether it was washing cars or making coffee, I did not care once I kept the job.

With my first wage packet, I bought my first brand new pair of Levi's jeans and then fell in love with a suit in Pamela Scott's in Grafton Street. I asked the lady if I could pay off a few pounds each week on the suit. She agreed – and I remember making the final payment and collecting the outfit. I still have it after all those years!

Although I had been mad keen to get out of school, I went back to night college to further educate myself in shorthand, typing and bookkeeping.

A couple of years later, the company paid for my driving lessons and I got my first company car. I then started to collect and deliver cars to customers and dealers which I loved. It was quite daunting and challenging at first, particularly when most of the cars were very luxurious. But I soon became a good driver; with the tight spots I often had to get in and out of, and being a woman in a male-dominated industry, I was determined that I could do it!

Then the company decided to purchase a car transporter. This required someone in the company to obtain a Certificate of Professional Competence in Road Haulage Operations, which entailed passing an exam.

I decided to go for it! I was the only female with all the other male truck drivers on the course, which was tough: the modules included law, finance, management and road safety legislation. The hardest part was having to learn and understand the mechanics of the truck. But I persevered and was awarded a Certificate of Professional Competence in Road Haulage Operations.

As a result, I was then promoted to Transport Manager, which involved going to Dublin Docklands, checking and organising cars to be transported to the main distributors and dealers in Dublin and the rest of the country. The goal was to fill the transporter on both legs of the trip. I really loved the work.

HENRY'S EARLY CAREER

Living in the country surrounded by farms and not many houses, Henry was constantly out working. There was always plenty to be done. He loved working outside and driving different machines, so he left school after his Junior Cert to run his own business involving machines. He bought a second-hand JCB and worked locally digging foundations, all kind of groundworks, driveway, entrances and silage pits.

In 1975, Henry's parents decided to self-build a new house on the opposite side of the road from where they were living. Henry's Dad Fintan had a lot of experience in groundwork and foundations. He also had a lot of contacts and good tradesmen friends.

At school, Henry had loved mechanical drawing and maths; he was also very good at reading drawings. So he marked out the foundations for the new house and worked alongside the tradesmen. He was a very good listener and was so interested in learning from such experienced people that he really soaked up the information. He says he gained invaluable experience from working with the various tradesmen – bricklayers, plumbers and plasterers.

When the family decided to buy a new shed for the hay, cattle, and pigs, with part of it used to store the farm trucks and machines, Henry did all the groundwork and built a pit to carry out mechanical repairs; it was the first time they had covered-in space to do this.

Helping to build another few houses and extensions in the area, Henry found one job led to another. He really enjoyed the building work so, as his experience grew, he extended into shop renovations and house extensions.

When he was working on the building sites, Henry noticed a problem all the construction companies were experiencing: getting rid of the excess soil. He approached some farmers and asked them if they would be interested in soil to fill in and reclaim some of the poor areas on their farms. Then he approached some construction companies and agreed a price to remove the excess soil and clay which he then levelled in the farmers' fields. Both the construction companies and the farmers were happy and, of course, Henry was smiling because he was being paid by both and making money.

For extra pocket money, Henry had been dabbling in cutting and selling logs to the locals. One winter, he decided to go further afield and ventured down to Tallaght to try and sell more logs. He quickly learnt the importance of market research! When he finally picked up the courage to knock on the first door, a very nice lady appeared, and Henry asked if she was interested in buying some logs. Her reply was "Ah love, sure we've no chimney or fire. Just look on the roof"!

Coillte advertised a tender for 3,000 tons of timber thinnings. The price was very low because it all had to be drawn out manually as it wasn't viable to use machinery. Henry, along with one of his friends, decided to buy the timber and then sell the firewood commercially.

He was advised that a horse would be ideal to pull the timber out. Of course, he had no horse and very little funds – but Ballyfermot was full of horses. Henry's friend Finbarr knew a guy there called Micko, who sold logs, so Henry came to an agreement with him to rent a horse in exchange for logs which Micko would re-sell.

With his welding experience, Henry built a saw and used the family's old tractor to go to Glencullen Forest, cut the trees, trim them, and pull them out with the horse. He and his friend had fierce trouble between the tractor breaking down and the horse running off. They would be up there until all hours of the morning. His mother would have been literally saying the Rosary as there were no mobile phones or any way of communicating. When he delivered the logs to Micko in Ballyfermot, the trailers were lined up and Henry would unload so many bags onto each four-wheel horse cart and Micko then would deliver to his customers.

Henry was supplying a huge number of bags of logs at this stage, but it was extremely hard work and a lot of the timber is still in Glencullen many years later.

Back in the 1970s, motorcycle trials were held a few times in Lord Massy's estate beside Henry's home in Killakee. Henry immediately was fascinated at how the competitors could ride up and down the steps of the Massys' home. He pestered his parents to buy him a bike. They didn't want to and bought him a lawn mower instead!

So he cut grass for the locals and later bought his own bike from his earnings. Two of his brothers then bought bikes.

Henry competing on his trials bike.

My six brothers – ready to compete!

The three O'Kelly brothers quickly were pretty much on par with my six brothers, fighting each weekend for titles in the motorcycle trials championships.

DATING HENRY

Henry asked me out on a few occasions while I was completing the course for my CPC, but I was so involved in pursuing my career that I had no interest in the distraction of dating.

Because both families knew each other well through the motorcycle trials, I was under pressure from some of my family to go out with Henry. They thought he was a great guy. So I agreed to one date – just to get them off my back!

On the Friday night I had agreed to meet Henry, I went for a quick drink with the lads from work and some of the guys from Nissan – which was a regular thing – and was asked to go for dinner by one of the owners of a main dealership. I would have accepted, only I had to meet Henry in Terenure at 8pm. I sat in my car outside the pub where we had agreed to meet. It was bucketing down, miserable, and dark – and Henry never arrived. I had never been stood up before – and I had just turned down a dinner date. I was hopping mad!

Henry called two days later. Apparently, he had got his nights mixed up. I still don't know to this day how I agreed to go out with him again! Fortunately, I did, and we continued to date.

Henry used to drive an old Land Rover which he loved. It was a banger, full of rattles and leaks. I dreaded going out in it as I had my lovely new company car, but I thought I better not offend him!

I'll never forget one trip to Cork for a two-day 4X4 trial, when we had to drive the Land Rover that Henry was competing in down and back in the height of the winter in October. The heater didn't work. There were holes in the floor with the wind blowing through. And there was no radio, so you could hear every rattle and bang out of it.

As we were approaching Nenagh, I said to Henry, "I can't go any further. We need to book into a hotel". At this stage, I did not care about the cost; I just needed to get some heat into myself.

It was late in the evening when we pulled up outside a hotel in the main street in Nenagh. Henry wanted to be able to park the Land Rover directly outside, so he could see it and make sure it was safe. He was afraid it was going to be stolen. "You could leave the doors open with the key in the ignition and it still would not be stolen," I said.

Henry's Land Rover competing in a 4X4 trial … and wading through muddy water.

Henry was known for his Land Rover breaking down in the trials. He started day one and after a few sections the halfshaft broke. A local competitor told him of a guy in Midleton who could fix it, so down we went. It was freezing cold, snowing, wet and miserable, but we had no choice as the Land Rover was our only way of getting home. So, while all the other competitors were enjoying dinner back at the hotel, we were stuck in the middle of nowhere, in what turned out to be a Funeral Undertaker's. Eventually, we got back to the hotel and had a few hours' sleep.

Back out onto the track the next morning, Henry won the second day's race. So at least we got to bring a trophy home. But we then had the dreaded trip back to Dublin, which took hours and was almost as bad as the trip down.

Henry with his winner's trophy.

As we got to know each other better, Henry and I realised we both had the same dream to start our own business. We were both working very hard and spending long hours pursuing our careers and so we kept the relationship very casual.

The company I worked for – Michael Orr Group – had become hugely successful with various branches and car dealerships. Most of the customers were very wealthy. I was very fortunate to have the opportunity to collect and deliver cars to the mansion houses that they lived in. I still remember deciding that this was the lifestyle I wanted. I was in my early 20s at the time and knew then that I wanted to:

- Set up my own business.
- Own a Range Rover.
- Own a sports convertible, working my way up to a Porsche.
- Own a house in the mountains, not too far from the city.
- Own a house abroad, preferably in America.
- Marry an entrepreneur with a similar dream.
- Have a few children who would continue my legacy.

I reckoned all I needed to do was keep working hard, educating myself, listening and learning from other successful entrepreneurs.

However, in the early 1980s, recession hit and a lot of motor companies went out of business. Unfortunately, the company I worked with was one of them. Liquidators were appointed and I was made redundant. I received a cheque for £975 statutory redundancy for 11 years' service! Michael Orr was very unfortunate. He had built a great business, had a great reputation and was very well respected in the industry.

So I spent the first 11 years of my career seeing first-hand how to start a business, grow it, employ people, borrow money, finance the business, make money, have a lavish lifestyle, and then lose it all! It was an invaluable experience.

Luckily, I was re-employed immediately by another main dealer.

A couple of years later, I moved to help set up another garage with Gordon Kellett, who I had worked with in Michael Orr's.

THE SAWMILL

O'KELLY'S SAWMILL

O'Kelly's Sawmill began when two guys approached Henry to rent part of the hayshed, as they wanted to buy a saw machine and set up a sawmill. Henry agreed: it was an easy way of making money, but also because he was very interested to see how they would get on given his own interest in timber.

The two guys had borrowed £20,000 to set up the business. They bought a second-hand log saw for around £6,000 but it took them months to set it up. By the time they were ready to begin trading, most of their borrowed money was gone and the cheques for rent soon began to bounce.

When Henry went back with a bounced cheque, they would take out a big cheque book and write another cheque. This went on for a couple of months until eventually Henry had enough and said, "There's no point in writing out another cheque to bounce!" It was obvious they had no money left. So Henry offered to buy the log saw and a deal was done.

Henry spent a couple of hours a day cutting timber planks and post and rail fencing which he managed to sell to local farmers. But there weren't enough orders to make money out of it. It then dawned on him that if he made something out of the timber, he would make a much higher margin than simply selling planks. The advantage of making a finished product like the panels and sheds was that there were multiple amounts of timber pieces used rather than one piece; hence the sale value and profit was higher. That's when he started to make his own fencing panels and later went on to making garden sheds.

Henry saw great potential for this type of business and decided to concentrate on the timber business and set up his own company in 1986: O'Kelly's Sawmill.

While Henry had a vast amount of experience, he had very little money. The only things he owned were "Amy", an old red Massey Ferguson 1200 tractor, and the log saw.

Amy was a great-looking tractor but gave him a lot of trouble: the steering kept jamming. Eventually out of desperation, he decided to disconnect the steering wheel and use a lever: to go right, you pulled the lever up, and to go left, you pulled it down. The steering wheel remained in place simply for aesthetics!

Henry moving logs drawn down from the forest, with Amy, the old red tractor, on the right.

Fortunately, Henry was good at welding. He bought a second-hand double-decker car transporter for £80. His friend Philip brought it to the yard for another £20. Henry cut it up and sold the top ramps to a local farmer. He then welded on a tow hitch to the bottom part of the car transporter and a log-lifting crane to use to load the logs in the forest.

When Henry went to the woods, Coillte would have drawn the logs from the forest to the side of the road. He would pick out which logs he wanted. The Coillte forester would then measure them by the cubic metre so Henry would know how much it was costing. He would have to write a cheque for the forester before he could take the timber.

Henry's friend Finbar helped cut the logs in the yard but Henry was looking for extra hands. One morning, three guys showed up in an old mustard-coloured Datsun looking for work. One was Adrian, who is now our General Manager over 30 years later. The others were Micheal, Adrian's brother-in-law, and Mick, a friend – all from Kildare.

As they got busier, Henry was going to the forest two to three times a week. He recalls how much he loved driving up the mountains first thing in the morning, being out in the fresh air. He also found the whole process very satisfying, from cutting the timber down, loading it with the tractor and trailer, bringing it back to re-cut into various lengths of timber to make into sheds and fence panels.

Later, as the business grew and more people were employed, his time was spent more and more in the office. He says, "I'd go into the office every morning to a pile of paperwork. I'd leave in the evening still with a pile of paperwork – with nothing to show for it. No sweating or inhaling the fresh air. No satisfaction. It's just something that had to be done".

The saw he had – a band rack saw – was mainly for cutting large logs and wasn't designed to cut fine boards for making the sheds. Ideally, he needed a resaw which would be much more efficient at cutting the timber into smaller sizes suitable for sheds and fencing – but resaws were very expensive.

At the time, there was a Woodworking Exhibition in the RDS. Henry went and, to his surprise, Stenner had the exact resaw he needed on display on their stand. Henry managed to negotiate a great deal with them; he was fortunate that Stenner didn't want to transport the machine back to the UK.

Henry was confident the bank would lend him the £10,810 he needed to buy the saw. It was a no brainer! The business was going well, and the new saw would be much more efficient as it could cut the boards four to five times quicker, which would increase the production of panels and, in turn, would improve profits. However, the bank turned down the loan. So Henry approached his cousin who said, "No problem" and wrote out a cheque there and then. Henry and the lads installed the machine themselves to save money.

Henry built a small room in the corner of the shed for an office and canteen. Because there was a lot of noise from the saw in the shed, he packed the wall with sawdust to try and block it out. But when they'd close the door of the canteen, the sawdust would come out of the wall.

Tea-break in the hayshed canteen – Henry, Adrian and Mick about to watch the match!

There were great stories to be told from that canteen. Henry recalls that they had field mice running around, since basically the shed was in the middle of a field. Micheal and Adrian constantly lost their lunch to the mice. So they put down traps and were delighted when they caught a mouse. They would empty it out and reset the trap. When they came back, there was another mouse caught. This went on for a while; they were thrilled to be catching so many mice. What they didn't realise was that one of lads, Mulligan, was taking the dead mice they threw out and putting them back in the trap. Eventually, Micheal and Adrian copped on when one day Mulligan put two mice in the one trap, head-to-head with a piece of cheese!

When Henry's parents, Fintan and Joan, sold their house across the road from the sawmill, Bob and Marlene moved in. Bob had retired from being a salesman in a steel company. He was an absolute gentleman – very experienced and polished, unlike the lads in the sawmill. From popping in for a chat, he took an interest in the business and started helping the lads. He always wore old dungarees and cap.

I looked after the finances of the sawmill, while continuing my fulltime job in the motor trade. Although the business was doing well, money was always tight. I remember driving into the yard from work on Friday evenings when Henry would be in the canteen negotiating the wages with the lads. When he eventually agreed on a figure, he would go down to his brothers Fintan and Padraig, who were working for a contractor as plumbers, to borrow the money.

The shed sales continued to grow over the next few years. It was a very competitive industry, and timber was very expensive. The only way we could see to compete was to use less timber by cutting the boards thinner. But this created problems, as customers complained about the quality.

Our accountant advised us to improve the quality and design of the sheds and charge more; this way we would make more money. As a result, the shed sales continued to grow with no complaints over the price. O'Kelly's Sawmill stood out from the competitors and soon gained a reputation for quality and service.

Henry gave one of his younger cousins, Brian, a job fitting the sheds. When the lads nicknamed him "The Shed Man", Brian had one of his friends signwrite the truck with the name. Henry wasn't mad about the name, although it did bring a lot of new business. Over 30 years later, we still carry the name and are known as The Shed Man – particularly with customers who bought their sheds back then.

The new Shed Man livery.

The Shed Man gate signage.

The sawmill continued to expand its range, mainly by customers coming in and asking if we could make a product. Henry always said "Yes" to get the order – and then he'd figure it out afterwards with Adrian, Micheal and Mick.

On one occasion, a lady came in and asked if he could make a pergola. Henry had no idea what a pergola was or looked like, let alone how to make it. He had to go to the library to look it up as there was no Internet or Google then. In fact, Henry spent a lot of time in the library, going to exhibitions and reading magazines to research new products.

Fintan O'Kelly and his truck.

Henry's Dad, Fintan, had his own truck, which he drove for the council. He was semi-retired so as the sawmill got busier, he would do some deliveries.

The sawmill – always busy, inside and out.

TIP: It is better to provide top quality products with a superior customer service. This way you can charge more, make a profit, and have fewer complaints.

Henry recalls one day a customer came into the yard and placed a large order of timber to build a pigeon house. Fintan delivered it to a beautiful big house in Rathmines. When he was carrying in the timber, he said to the customer, "Will you not have trouble with your neighbours building this big pigeon house?" "No, I won't", came the quick reply. Neither Henry nor his dad recognised that this guy was a well-known criminal! But he gave Fintan a £20 tip, which was a lot of money then! Fintan never let on to anyone who he was and allowed customers to think he was just the delivery man. This way, he got much better tips!

When the sawmill received an order to supply two miles of fencing panels at Dublin Airport, Fintan delivered the panels in an old green Land Rover and a trailer that Henry made up. He used to joke, "They'd think it was a 747 coming down the runway when they'd see me driving down the taxiway".

Micheal, Adrian and Con.

There was always great banter among the staff and the customers, which became part of the culture of the company. When a customer phoned asking if their order was ready, Bob would laugh and say,

"Not at all. It could be next week". Back then, the customers didn't seem to mind!

Although the sawmill was very much hidden on a narrow country road – there were no motorways or housing estates nearby, only local farmers – most of the customers at this stage came from word-of mouth and referrals, although the company also advertised in local newspapers.

Our children's colouring books.

Henry designed a book with sketches of our sheds, fencing, swings, with the lads making the products using their saws and tools. We gave copies of the book to the children to take home and colour in. It was a clever way of them showing the parents our product range.

OUR WEDDING

When my parents decided to sell their house, now in Moyne Road, Rathmines, they moved to Prosperous in Kildare – an hour's drive to and from work for me. More importantly, it was now costing Henry more money in diesel to travel up and down for a date! Being the smart guy that he is, Henry decided it would be better to marry me – he'd save on diesel and have a free bookkeeper!

So, in 1987, we started to build our new home on a site beside the sawmill. Henry designed the house: timber-framed with a basement. His Uncle John and his cousin Brian helped with the building. As any money we had needed to go into the business, the house was built on a very tight budget. We borrowed £20,000 from the bank. That barely covered the essentials, so we borrowed furniture from the family. Instead of a garden, the house was surrounded by timber and scrap!

I was so busy with my career that I hadn't time to spend days going to different stores to buy my wedding dress. My parents said they would go with me. I knew my Dad was dreading it as he didn't have the patience for shopping. But within a few hours, my dress and going away outfit were bought in the first two shops just off Grafton Street. Dad couldn't believe how easy it was!

Henry was my parents' fifth son-in-law and the favourite without doubt. Mum and Dad loved him and he had great respect for them. In our family, we were never allowed to curse in the house, but Henry could – and got away with it!

I was to finish work at 1pm on Friday the day before the wedding. That will tell you how dedicated I was to my career. I was under pressure trying to get everything finished. I had to make a bank lodgement and post letters on the way home. Accidentally, I posted the lodgement in the post box. Frantic, I contacted the post office and, to cut a long story short, I was passed through several people until eventually someone contacted the postman who was due to collect the letters to go to the sorting office. I met him at the post box and got the lodgement back!

To save money, Henry and I decided to rent a marquee and have the reception beside his family's home in Killakee. It never dawned on us what we would do if the weather was bad.

Our wedding marquee.

Henry's Mum and her neighbours offered to prepare the food. I remember going into the house after the post office fiasco to be met with the smell of eggs; there were hundreds being peeled, not to mention all the other food being prepared in the kitchen. Although they were typical country women, well used to cooking and baking, it was still a huge undertaking. One of the neighbours, Pascal, who owned a local pub, agreed to set up and run the bar. We hired a band and Henry's cousin Johnny, a well-known musician, played a few tunes.

*Our wedding day, with Janet Lindsay, my bridesmaid, and Fintan,
Henry's brother, as best man.*

6 August 1988 was a very special day as it was the first wedding in Henry's family and my family thought we'd never get married since Henry and I were so engrossed in our careers! The ceremony was in the beautiful old church in Beechwood Avenue, close by our previous home in Moyne Road, with almost 200 guests.

I was so busy working it never dawned on me to try on the dress before the wedding. Fortunately, my sister-in-law Yvonne was in the house the morning of the wedding when I discovered the hem needed to be sewn.

Padraig, Henry's brother, arrived in his dad's Mercedes to drive me to the church from the house in Prosperous. When we got to the Naas Road, Padraig suddenly pulled over at Newlands Cross and whipped me out of the back of the car into a fabulous vintage Bentley driven by Pat Denning, owner of the well-known Denning's Garage.

We were very late because of the dress hem issue, so Pat tried to make up time. I remember the Bentley going around the Walkinstown roundabout on two wheels!

When we came out of the church, I realised Henry didn't know about the Bentley. Pat had decided to surprise us both. Pat drove us to Killakee with the sun beaming down on us from fabulous blue skies! It was 30 degrees.

Stepping out of the wedding Bentley.

In the marquee, Henry's Dad stood up to make his speech and got stuck for words. He said, "She's … she's a …" and had the guests in stitches laughing. Throughout the evening, the floor of the marquee started to sink. When the guests commented, we just said they were drunk!

Thankfully, it didn't rain as the marquee would have ended up in the bottom field! It was a fantastic wedding; everything went off brilliantly.

THE SAWMILL EXPANDS

When we returned from our honeymoon in Bulgaria, I returned to my job in the motor industry while looking after the accounts for the sawmill. Although the turnover was low, as was the profit, the potential was there to grow the business.

As the sawmill grew and added more staff, it was time to move away from the small office / canteen in the shed. So Henry bought a second-hand 40ft shipping container with plywood sides on it.

Our new sales office – an old shipping container – being manoeuvred into place.

The yard wasn't level, so Henry got 40-gallon oil drums and cut the top and bottom off them which gave him eight legs, stood two of them on top of each other, and filled them with concrete. Some of the reps from the timber suppliers worried whether it was safe!

Finished stock of fencing and timber products at the sawmill.

Liam, who previously worked for a well-known merchant provider locally, joined the company and brought great experience to the business. He was extremely mannerly, well-groomed and a perfectionist which we didn't have in the business at the time.

Con, Liam and Adrian in the sawmill.

The sawmill was contracted to make special pallets for satellite dishes that were being exported around the world. We were also supplying pallets and crates to various other companies, which was a very competitive business. But we had built up a lot of nice steady accounts with different civil engineering companies.

We were now selling fencing posts, panels, goal posts, pegs, decking, sheds, furniture, gates and swings and slides. and custom-made products to both the general public and trade customers.

LEAVING THE MOTOR TRADE

I had signed up for a Diploma in Motor Industry Management. The course was two evenings a week for two years in DIT, Bolton Street, covering Law, Management, Accountancy and Administration & Organisation in Service, Parts & Sales Divisions. All the students were all male except one other girl.

Gordon Kellett Services Ltd. are pleased to announce the appointment of Shirley O'Kelly to the position of General Manager from July 1st 1990.

I found it very hard going as my days were always so demanding in the garage and then going straight to college in the evening. It had been a long time since I was in school, so I found the homework hard – and there was a lot of it. I was also looking after the accounts for the sawmill.

But a year later, I was appointed General Manager of Gordon Kellett Services.

I also became a member of the Porsche Club GB (my dream car!)

Unfortunately, Henry's Dad, Fintan, passed away in 1990 after a short illness. Soon after, I announced I was pregnant with the first O'Kelly grandchild.

I was six months pregnant when, on 4 June, I didn't feel well. I put it down to being tired with work and college. That evening, I had to go to college as the lecturers were going back over the previous two years' work before the final exams a week later. Unfortunately, during class, I felt much worse.

I drove myself to Mount Carmel Hospital, where my twin boys were born prematurely that night. Looking back, I realise I obviously went into complete shock, as the Rotunda Hospital was right beside the college.

By the time Henry arrived, the boys had just died. The doctor said their hearts weren't developed enough to survive. I said it was nice that I got to hold them alive.

We buried them in a small white coffin and named them after the two Grandads, Fintan and Ernest.

Dr. Murphy explained it was one of those unfortunate things and advised me to go and get pregnant again as I was perfectly healthy.

But first, I had to sit my final exams. I sat them alone under supervision in the college. I graduated and received my Diploma in Motor Industry Management in addition to a Technician Certificate in Transport Engineering.

A few months later, I became pregnant again.

At this stage, I had been looking after the sawmill's finances for the past five years. Henry noticed there was a good growth in the domestic market as people had more disposable income and were showing a lot more interest in their gardens. People were turning more to wood. Its appearance plays a major role, as it's softer on the eye than the alternatives and looks more natural.

We recognised the potential to grow the business further and take advantage of the trend towards wood by placing a lot more emphasis on the product range and quality, which enabled us to charge more. However, it required me to work full-time in the sawmill to allow Henry to concentrate on operations.

So I decided to leave the motor trade, although I had worked my way up to Transport Manager and on to General Manager. I would have loved to have run my own motor company, but would have been too reliant on mechanics even though I had a lot of experience. I believe that if you're setting up a business it's important to know, understand and be able to do everything yourself.

It was a very difficult decision to make as I had worked with Gordon Kellett for a long time. He and Muriel were very good to me and had become great friends.

I absolutely loved every single day of working in the motor industry. I had gained tremendous experience in every aspect of the trade, having been very fortunate with the opportunity of working with three different businesses from the early start-up stage.

I worked with and met great people along the way. And working in such a male-dominated industry and being faced with so many challenges made me a very focused and determined person.

In leaving the motor trade, the reality was that I was giving up:

- A very nice salary that was guaranteed each week.
- A free company car that was replaced regularly.
- The chance of driving various luxurious cars and other perks like travel and dining out.

I also had a mortgage and a child on the way.

This was scary enough to make me even more determined to succeed! I recall driving into the sawmill yard the day I left the motor trade. I stood there, pregnant, thinking "This had better work"! All I'd left behind to join a new business with my husband, with very little money, a hayshed and the old red tractor Amy!

Then I remembered why I was doing this: to follow my dream. I knew I wanted to:

- Set up my own business.
- Own a Range Rover.
- Own a sports convertible, working my way up to a Porsche.
- Own a house in the mountains, not too far from the city.
- Own a house abroad, preferably in America.
- Marry an entrepreneur with a similar dream.
- Have a few children who would continue my legacy.

Henry's dream was the same as mine, except he wanted to own a helicopter rather than the cars. He used to watch them flying over his house to and from Baldonnell and always had a keen interest.

We had gained a lot of experience through our hard work over the years. We were both reared with very little money and were not prepared to take out any unnecessary loans, but with passion and determination we were prepared to put in the effort to build a very successful business to achieve our dreams.

With the housing boom in 1993, we secured our first contract with a builder – Castlethorn Construction – to supply and fit fencing between the gardens on a new housing estate. This was followed by more contracts with other builders – with up to 300 gardens to be fenced in some cases.

Henry's previous experience was an advantage here, as he was used to pricing jobs, and he was very good at mechanical drawing and maths. He would measure on site the cubic metres of timber needed and then work out how much concrete and how many panels were required.

Garden fencing was great advertising for the company as we fitted a badge on every panel with our details for people to see while they were viewing the showhouses.

While carrying out market research, one product stood out: noise barrier fencing. We secured our first job at Donnybrook Bus Station, followed by contracts on other sites, including the M50.

Business was going from strength to strength. We had moved on from the mucky yard, old hayshed, and Amy the tractor! The profits were invested in the business to build a new showroom, tarmac the car park, and fit front entrance gates and signage.

We also created a display of our sheds surrounded by trees on the edge of the forest. With Henry's experience in building, we have always been able to carry out renovations and improvements on the premises ourselves which saved us a lot of money.

However, all was not plain sailing; there were a few problems. Business slowed down over the winter months, cashflow became tight as a large percentage of the turnover was tied up in trade credit accounts and the company was heavily reliant on builders. We decided we needed to generate more business through the domestic market. This was

TIMBER
&
SHED SPECIALIST

O'Kelly's Sawmill is situated in the
foothills of the Dublin Mountains,
(Just below the Hell Fire Club),
Overlooking Dublin Bay.

Call in and see our display
Mon - Fri 9.00 am - 5.30 pm
Sat 9.00 am - 4.00 pm

PERGOLA TOP FENCING

Tel : 493 1034   Fax : 493 4406

challenging as most people in the new housing estates built nearby thought we were just a small timber yard dealing with the trade.

The display area for our timber products.

Our Mission Statement: The success of the business will be based on differentiation through innovative design, quality materials and craftmanship, in addition to superior customer service. Henry will concentrate on the operational side of the business, while Shirley will concentrate on the finances and administration.

MAGNETS

Prior to leaving the motor trade, I had come across fridge magnets while visiting Henry's cousin in New York. Their fridge door was full of magnets advertising different types of business – the local hairdresser, dentist, etc. I thought this was a great way of advertising.

I did some research and decided to set up my own little venture alongside the sawmill business, selling advertising magnets. I used the slogan: "Don't lick, don't peel. Just place on steel".

Henry researched the equipment we would require to make the magnets. One of his cousins who was experienced in computers showed him what he needed to know. We purchased an Apple Mac computer to design the magnets, as well as a vinyl cutter and a second-hand die-cutting machine. We imported the sheets of magnets from the USA. Henry had a better understanding of the software and machines than I had; he also went to the library to learn how to screenprint, along with educating himself on the Apple Mac. Later, we took on an experienced employee.

We made up a sample pack of magnets and sent a mail shot to several large multinational companies. The first two orders we received were from Cow & Gate and Persil: 250,000 magnets each, which was worth £15,000. We also received some orders with smaller quantities.

We designed a magnet in the shape of a tooth and I dropped samples into the local dentist practices. We received a lot of orders. We also secured orders from RTÉ, Guinness, Milupa – all great names to have in our portfolio.

We sold a magnet in the shape of a signpost with the various counties to retail outlets. And then we supplied vehicle magnets which were very convenient if you didn't want to have your company name on your van or car outside work hours.

Promotional Magnets
Self Adhesive Magnetic Strip
Magnetic Data Card Holder

TEL: 493 7026
FAX: 493 4406

MAGNET
ADVERTISING

Magnet Supplies & Advertising Limited
Killakee, Rathfarnham, Dublin 16.

Phone : 01 493 7026
Fax : 01 493 4406

54 x 25 mm

Price
S

68 mm Round

Price
B

41 x 70 mm

Price
A

41 x 70 mm

Price
A

68 X68 mm

Price
B

85 x 5

Price
B

60 x 50 mm

Price
A

We can make
other Shapes.
Cost of die to
cut out shape
approx 380.00
euro Plus VAT

80 x 60 mm
Oval

Price
B

43

We prepared the artwork to be screenprinted, got plates made for the shape of the magnet which then we had to die-cut with our machine. Then the magnets were packed in individual plastic bags with a Magnet Advertising sticker on the back and a paper insert with the client's message.

There was always a tight deadline on the orders. Danielle and Ciara their childhood evenings spent watching Disney movies while working through a pile of magnets. They said even the babysitter and some of their friends were roped in! My brother Keith reminded me of a time he visited my Mum and Dad for afternoon tea with his wife Yvonne and their children; they ended up packing magnets – 4,000 to be exact!

Cow & Gate and Milupa's orders were repeated several times with large quantities each time. I was thrilled with the repeat orders – though the kids and family were less enthusiastic! We also supplied rolls of magnetic strip which was adhesive on one side and magnetic on the other. This was a very popular product used in a lot of schools. In fact, we were contracted by an educational supply company to make fractions and decimals for schools. This was a very good contract which ran for years.

Although it was a great business and a nice injection of money, it was time-consuming. In the end, although we closed the business after a couple of years, Magnet Advertising allowed me to achieve one of my dreams, as we were now able to afford a second-hand Range Rover.

Henry's 4X4 Land Rover was used to promote Magnet Advertising.

DANIELLE ARRIVES

Danielle was born in July 1992, in Mount Carmel Hospital.

As the doctor was monitoring my pregnancy closely, he had arranged for me to be admitted on Friday, 17 July. I phoned the hospital asking if I could come in at 3pm instead of 1pm, as I still had work to finish off. They said, "No!" When I checked in, I begged the nurse to let me sleep for a few hours as I was so tired from working. Again, she said, "No!" The doctor started the process of going into natural labour by walking me up and down the corridor. One of the joys of running your own business: no maternity leave!

Danielle was born on Saturday, 18 July, and everything went smoothly – at first. Coincidently, my parents had a family party in their house that day, so Henry only had to make one phone call rather than 11 to give them the good news.

Then suddenly all hell broke loose. I started to haemorrhage. Dr. Murphy was called back in with his team of nurses. Every time they thought they had the bleeding under control, it started again – and again. They kept giving me epidurals. Eventually, it all settled down and Dr. Murphy went home reassuring Henry and myself that everything was OK. An hour later, he was back and this time I remember saying "Just leave me to die". I was in so much pain and so worn out, I couldn't take anymore. I was moved to theatre. Thankfully, by some miracle, I pulled through.

None of the family on either side were aware of anything as it all happened so fast.

A few weeks later, Danielle was christened, followed by a big party in the barn. It was a huge celebration particularly for the O'Kelly's – Danielle was their first grandchild.

As soon as she could walk, Danielle was working!

SANTA COMES TO THE SAWMILL

Henry and I were sitting by the fire one evening trying to think of how to attract more people into the sawmill to increase sales and free up cashflow. Suddenly, I said to Henry, "I have a great idea!"

"What is it?" said Henry.

"Santa!"

He thought I was joking – and then realised I was very serious.

We had the ideal setting in the Dublin mountains on the edge of the forest. The sheds, treehouses and fence panels were already on display, surrounded by trees.

Being parents ourselves, we knew it had to be perfect and that the children would have to believe this was the real Santa in the Dublin mountains.

Henry didn't know it at the time, but I didn't see this as being a once-off event! I really felt this could be a great way of attracting potential customers every year to the business.

We decorated the outdoor display with coloured lights. We bought artificial reindeers made from plywood and hired amplifiers, which we hung from the trees, to play traditional Christmas songs. We converted the showrooms and stores inside into a Santa Village, consisting of Santa's kitchen, bedroom and workshop, which were all traditionally decorated. We also had live birds, sheep and deer from local farmers and a snow scene with stuffed characters like Barney, Snow White and other Disney characters.

Bob, our neighbour, was the perfect build for Santa and his wife Marlene was perfect for Mrs. Claus. Danielle and Ciara, and some of the neighbours' children, were the elves, while Henry's Mum was in Santa's kitchen baking.

Santa arrives at the sawmill, with elf helpers Danielle and Ciara!

The Christmas scene, in among the shed display.

Everyone enjoying seeing Santa.

Santa came out of the treehouse and was met by Mrs. Claus. He shook hands with the children as he walked down through the display of sheds and fencing … which they loved. When the children visited Santa in his room, the elf behind the chimney dropped the present down, which fascinated everyone.

Santa at O'Kelly's Sawmill was run over two weekends up to Christmas for four hours each day. We advertised it with flyers on notice boards in the nearby shops, schools, and community centres.

Two hundred children, plus their parents, visited Santa that first year. We received incredible feedback, so Santa was coming back the next year!

Every year, it got busier and busier – to the point where we were worried about the length of time people were queuing as it was so cold in the mountains at that time of the year. The customers didn't seem to mind because they were all singing and dancing to the Christmas songs while they were served mulled wine and mince pies and the children played in the sheds.

Our first Santa flyer – an early use of emojis in advertising.

Bob and Ned preparing for Santa's arrival.

We decided to build on extra two rooms with another two Santas (two employees who were "persuaded"!). We made sure the rooms were decorated the same in case families were showing photos afterwards. We built moving walls with doors so no one would cop on – it was perfect!

At all the corporate Christmas parties and socialising, one of the conversations was generally, "Where do you take your children to see Santa?". Of course, O'Kelly's Sawmill came up a lot.

By the sixth year, we had almost 7,000 children, plus adults, visit Santa over three weekends. People travelled from all over the country – and even from abroad – to visit Santa at the sawmill, which was not down to advertising, merely word-of-mouth. The whole experience of driving up the mountains, being met by the big Santa sign at the gate and the music playing before they even got out of the car was so magical for the children. The atmosphere was brilliant; we really did succeed in putting on a memorable day for everyone. Most people said it was the next best thing to Lapland!

Henry and I were totally blown over with the success of the event. However, we were really worried there was going to be an accident. The country road couldn't accommodate the parking and our own yard wasn't big enough. A lot of people would come late in the afternoon, as it was even more magical in the dark. So we made the difficult decision to discontinue the event in the interest of safety.

More fun with Santa and Mrs. Claus!

The following year we emailed customers to explain the situation. Although they were disappointed, they also understood. For the next few years, we were still taking phone calls from customers hoping we were bringing Santa back.

With so many people working at the event – staff, friends, and neighbours – we didn't really make any money. However, we successfully displayed our products over three weekends to thousands of parents, grandparents and friends of the children who came to see Santa. All had cameras taking photos and videos of our products with our business name displayed.

Henry's mum, Joan, working in Santa's kitchen!

Looking back, I think one of the reasons Santa at O'Kelly's Sawmill was so successful was because it wasn't commercialised like other places. We weren't trying to sell sheds or fencing on the day, as we were conscious it was a special family day out. Our priority was to give a memorable experience to everyone who attended. We were confident the sales would come after.

And they did! The turnover increased dramatically over the following years. Everyone was talking about Santa at O'Kelly's Sawmill. They're still talking about it – every winter, we get phone calls asking if Santa is coming back – which proves the success of Santa!

CIARA & CONOR

In 1995, our second daughter, Ciara, was born. This time, everything went smoothly and I was back in the office five days later – again, no maternity leave! There was just no one to delegate the work to.

Ciara loved her sleep, which suited me as I was able to get more work done while she slept in the cot next to me in my office. We had to juggle a lot, trying to rear two children along with running the sawmill and Magnet Advertising. Every night was dinner, children to bed and back to work until all hours trying to keep on top of everything!

Multi-tasking at the kitchen table – notice the high-tech cabling!

In 1997, our son, Conor, was born. Again, thankfully all went according to plan. He was the first grandson for Henry's Mum and the 21st grandchild for my parents. Again a few days later, back to work, no maternity leave!

Just over a year later, I had a hysterectomy. We felt very lucky that Danielle, Ciara, and Conor were all healthy. I recall being very ill for a

short while and then back on my feet faster than most others as there was still no one to delegate the work to!

I have always said that the only way I could describe Conor was "a child that couldn't grow up fast enough". As soon as he started to walk, I had terrible trouble trying to keep him in the house. Living beside the sawmill, he was always looking out the window at the lads and machines working. Any chance he got, he was gone – out through a hedge or under the gate – and then I would have the lads running around looking for him. He started to drive machines from a very young age.

A WINNING STREAK!

The company was getting stronger and stronger and had built up a good reputation. We had invested in trucks, diggers, a forklift, and various other equipment required to carry out the work. Henry recalls that when he wanted to buy a machine or truck, he would have to justify to me how we would make money from it before I would agree to financing anything. Not that Henry was reckless with money – after all, everything we owned was second-hand!

In 1997, the company was awarded Outright Winner in the Timber Products category in the Irish Forestry Awards. This was the company's first award – and a very prestigious one! It was great exposure for the business.

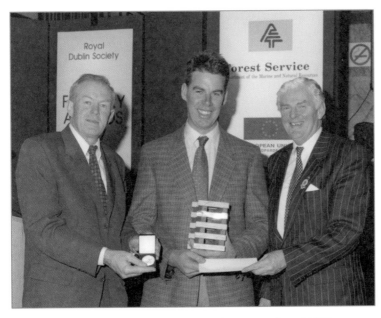

Henry being presented with the Irish Forestry Award 1997.

In 1998, Henry surprised me with a newer model Range Rover for my birthday. I was totally stunned! We had family and friends over for dinner when he handed me a small box with the keys in it. He had hidden the Range Rover, with balloons tied onto it, behind the house.

The surprise birthday Range Rover!

The company continued going from strength to strength. We were now supplying the construction sector, landscaping contractors, local authorities and the domestic market. Providing the full range of services from site survey, fence design and manufacture to erection gave us a unique competitive advantage in the market. We had successfully gained a reputation for top quality products with superior customer service.

Henry's role was starting to change to spending more time behind the computer in his office as he was the person to carry out the site survey, design special features for the site, figure out the materials required and the cost. We were locked into most of our contracts for between one and three years, so it was imperative to get the price and costing accurate.

The yard and shed departments were easy to organise, as it was all operated on site. There was a lot more involved in organising installations – and there were more expenses involved such as machinery, tools, trucks, diesel, insurance, and maintenance, not to mention wages.

If three or four builders were looking for the lads, they'd be trying to juggle between sites. Then sometimes the lads would arrive on site to do an installation and the builder wouldn't be ready. There was a lot of moving diggers between sites and then getting the panels and concrete to arrive on time. Of course, the weather was a huge factor so the lads wouldn't have been as productive over the winter months.

An advertisement we placed in The Irish Times.

Henry worked long hours trying to catch up, as he was still spending a lot of time in the yard and on site – and we were getting a lot of orders for bespoke products which Henry had to be involved with.

We had our annual meeting with the bank that we – and Henry's parents – had been banking with for years. We were looking forward to the meeting as we had increased our sales and profits on the previous year, which was partially due to new contracts secured with builders.

But when the bank manager went through the annual accounts and noticed some builders outstanding on the debtors listing, he got very upset with us and remarked, "Why are you getting involved with builders and giving credit? It's too risky". I explained how the builders completed a credit application form and how we had checked out the credit references. We also agreed credit terms in writing before starting work – and to date we hadn't had an issue with payments, nor were we concerned. I explained to the manager that the figures he was looking at weren't even yet due for payment. He still wasn't happy!

Next thing, he noticed another amount outstanding, which was for a treehouse we had fitted the previous week. When he saw the name beside it, he said we would be lucky to get paid!

Henry had been collecting money since his early years and I had also spent years in the motor trade and the sawmill being responsible for collecting debtors and keeping accounts up-to-date. I had always kept a tight control – and still do.

So when we left the bank, we decided to chance calling to the customer's house with the hope of picking up a cheque. Luckily, as we pulled up the couple were at the gate waving visitors goodbye. To be fair, as we expected, they wrote out the cheque there and then.

We returned to the bank later that day to lodge the cheque. The manager happened to be standing at the counter. I handed him the cheque. He took it and said, "I'll be surprised if this doesn't bounce". I marched out of the bank without saying anything I was so disgusted with him. We had to wait five days to confirm the cheque went through – which it did.

On another occasion, we received an enquiry from a customer to build a specialised shed/building. Henry made up the drawings with the price and was delighted when the order was confirmed. All these bespoke orders were great for the company's portfolio. But when I went looking for payment, the customer would only pay a small amount off the bill at a time, saying that he wanted more work done. Although I kept the pressure on, this went on for a while.

Eventually, I wrote to the customer in early December, requesting the balance be paid in full by close of business before Christmas; if he failed to do so, we would be at his house to take back the shed/building on 2 January when we re-opened.

Despite the fact he had told Henry he was delighted with the work, we didn't get paid. So, on 2 January, Henry and Paddy loaded up the trucks with the chainsaws and headed to the house. They drove around the back to the shed. Henry said to Paddy, "Get up on the roof and start the chainsaw", thinking that, once the customer heard the noise, he would come out and hand over a cheque.

They got that wrong! Instead, the customer came out pointing a gun at the roof and fired a shot! Henry and Paddy couldn't believe it.

Later, we issued legal proceedings to get the full amount of money owed, which was approximately €7,000. Eventually a settlement was made. At least, we tried!

Henry had a natural flair for design. His expertise in mechanical drawing, together with his experience of ground preparation, building and drainage, were critical factors in the provision of children's playgrounds.

Dublin Zoo approached us to design and build play units that would complement the different animals in various areas of the Zoo. Henry submitted his drawings, which included a climbing frame and ring swings for the children to swing on as they watched the monkeys beside them swinging. For the elephants, we made an elephant slide and, for the seals, we built slippy slides.

Henry carried out extensive research into playgrounds. He also researched the health and safety regulations, which involved trips to workshops in the UK to ensure we met all the relevant safety standards. The response was tremendous, which led to numerous other contracts resulting from the display in Dublin Zoo with our company name on it. Sales increased dramatically: picnic tables, benches, swing, slides and treehouses. We secured contracts with hotels and caravan parks around the country, including Fota Wildlife, Blarney Park Hotel and Mayo County Council.

Bunratty Folk Park contacted us wanting something different. So Henry suggested a miniature castle and maze which they loved.

The maze at Bunratty Folk Park – and the Adventure Play area at Fota Wildlife Park.

Henry and Kaspars standing beside the elephant slide at Dublin Zoo.

Adventure Playground contracts at Dublin Zoo and Fota Island

O'KELLYS have an unequalled reputation for ionnovative design and high standards of craftsmanship in timber playground products.

The range is in constant development to meet the diverse requirements of specifiers - designers, architects and builders, as well as new trends in the wider consumer market. Products are designed for aesthetic appeal with function, longevity and safety in mind.

ADVENTURE PLAYGROUND products are an O'Kelly specialisation. In recent years the company has built a unique expertise in the design and building of playground facilities. The company has undertaken public projects including major commissions to design and install playgrounds at Dublin Zoo and at Fota Island.

O'KELLYS SUPPLY AN EXTENSIVE RANGE OF PRODUCTS IN:

FENCING is made in a variety of styles to complement both traditional and modern environments. Many have specific functions – such as sound reduction or soil retention for sloping sites.

TIMBER BUILDINGS range from sturdy garden sheds to wendy houses and highly attractive tree houses that will have dads returning to their childhood!

Heading into 2000, the house-building boom was in full swing. The company had built up a strong customer base among many of the country's top builders and developers. We supplied them with garden sheds and fencing. Everything was going very well.

But with our home beside the sawmill overlooking the yard, it was virtually impossible to switch off and have time to think. Henry and I would generally end up working when everyone was gone home.

We had been to Florida a few times and loved it. We decided to buy a house there while the children were at an age to enjoy Disney. The plan was to rent it out to cover the mortgage and expenses until we would be in a better position to use it more ourselves.

Danielle, Ciara and Conor on Henry's Honda Goldwing motorcycle at our Florida home.

With the way technology was developing, we knew it was only a matter of time when we would be able to work from there. Back then we were able to dial into our server in Ireland to access the accounts and wages; however, it was very slow and tedious. Now we have full access to everything, we can even talk with the guys and customers / suppliers on our landline extension, so no one knows where we are working from. It's seamless!

TIP: Listen to your bank manager and then go with your gut! Luckily, we did – or we wouldn't have had the sales and profits from the builders.

Looking back, it's clear that our success was based on innovation and diversification, along with top quality workmanship and superior customer service. We created a unique experience for the customer when they visited our premises. We worked very hard together and made a great team with our 25 employees to achieve just over £1.5m in sales. Henry was still focused on the manufacturing, while I was focused on the finances and administration and rearing our three children.

So by 2000, I had achieved some of my dreams!

- The house in the mountains.
- Married to a successful entrepreneur.
- Three healthy children.
- A second-hand Range Rover.
- The house in Florida.

TURNING A NEGATIVE INTO A POSITIVE

In 2002, there was an insurance crisis in Ireland with huge increases in premiums. O'Kelly's Sawmill had been insured with Lloyds of London since 1986. But when we went to renew our policy, we were informed by our insurance broker that Lloyds was pulling out of Ireland.

The broker approached all the insurance companies. None was even prepared to quote, despite the fact we had no history of claims over our 16 years of cover.

We were within 48 hours of the insurance expiring and were terrified that we were going to have to close the business down. We simply couldn't operate without insurance, particularly given the nature of the business.

O'Kelly's Sawmill was a member of the Small Firms Association, part of IBEC. So I contacted Pat Delaney, who was then the Director, and explained the situation. I was literally crying on the phone. He could hear how upset and worried I was about having to cease business. Pat contacted Hibernian Insurance, who agreed to meet us in the sawmill. Although we were delighted with this progress, we knew we were in a very vulnerable situation and that Hibernian could literally name their price – which they did. Our premium increased from €22,000 to €75,000 for 12 months, which excluded the product cover that was crucial for the business. Also bear in mind we had an additional premium to pay on our motor fleet policy for the trucks and machinery.

Henry and I sat down that evening trying to figure out what to do. First, we didn't have the money to pay €75,000 in insurance premiums. Second, even if we had the money, we couldn't fulfil orders for fitting playgrounds as Hibernian wouldn't give us product cover. We weren't prepared to operate without this cover as we were – always have been and still are – very safety-conscious.

I remember saying to Henry, "If we are going to close down our business, it will be for our own reasons. We can't let someone else force us out of business. We have worked so hard to build up a successful and profitable business from nothing to have it all taken away".

So we made the decision to borrow the money to pay the increased premium and go back and fight with Hibernian for the product cover we needed. The playground orders were worth a lot of money and the increase in the premium was bad enough without losing sales on top.

Insurance premium increases was big news at the time and the Small Firms Association ran several conferences with the main topic being the insurance crisis. The CEO of Hibernian was making a presentation at one of these SFA events. I decided to go to the conference, make myself known to him and plead our case.

I caught up with him at a coffee break and explained our situation. Of course, he didn't even know who O'Kelly's Sawmill was! I literally begged him to give us the product cover. He scheduled another meeting and eventually we succeeded in persuading Hibernian. However, of course, the critical product cover came with an additional premium! We were still going to lose money that year but at least we could fulfil the playground orders.

And then we turned a negative into a positive! A few days later, I was interviewed by Pat Kenny on RTÉ Radio about our situation with the insurance increase. When I finished, I went into the sales office and every line on the telephone board was ringing. I couldn't believe it; some people were placing orders and others were just congratulating us for fighting and not taking the easy route in closing the business. It was incredible, because January is normally our slow season and the phones would hardly ring.

Pat Kenny was followed by being interviewed on RTÉ News and TV3 News, live from the yard. We also featured in several newspapers and even made it into the New York Times!

In fairness to Hibernian, when they launched their new Riskasyst programme, they approached us to participate in a radio advert, along with a newspaper advert, followed by being on the front cover of Hibernian's yearbook. Henry and I were delighted to receive so much free advertising. But it only happened because we were determined to fight the insurance company.

TIP: It's important to get out of the office and network. Had we not been a member of the Small Firms Association, without the connections I don't know how we would have got the insurance.

Articles in five newspapers: Ireland on Sunday, The New York Times, The Sunday Times, The Sunday Tribune and The Star.

The positive: Hibernian Insurance advertising O'Kelly's Sawmill.

Sadly, even though we had been successful in obtaining product cover for playgrounds, we struggled against the competition. Larger companies with stronger revenues could produce very impressive catalogues, showing photos of their products with drawings and all the necessary health and safety specifications. They also had a library of files for each of their play units, which could be dragged and dropped into a new design drawing. This meant that, if an architect was asked to include a playground in a project, it was more convenient to drag and drop units into the drawing that had all the correct health and safety specifications. Then when the playground went for tender, all the designs and specifications were now leaning very much towards the bigger manufacturers who were set up to make multiple units, which is way more competitive than a small company trying to make one-off units to someone else's specifications.

The only way O'Kelly's Sawmill could have an advantage was if it was a specific design and build project like Dublin Zoo, Bunratty Castle or Fota Wildlife, where we produced our own design and drawings and built to the customer's specific needs. Despite this, the company continued to fit playgrounds for smaller businesses like crèches, which were still profitable.

PROFESSIONALISING THE BUSINESS

When I worked in the motor trade, at one stage I ran a service department, where labour was always the key cost. When I booked cars in for repairs, I would set up a job card, which was given to the mechanic, who would return it on completion of the work. The card itemised the parts fitted and labour used. This system ensured the payroll and parts were always charged to the customer.

In the sawmill, typically the customer would arrive in with a photo. Henry would then draw it on his computer to work out dimensions, material, and labour to quote a price. It was very difficult to get the price right as, in most cases, it was our first time to make the product.

So I implemented a job card system for the sawmill, which was particularly important as labour was also the key cost in our business and most of the orders were custom-made. Inputting the information into a spreadsheet then highlighted that we were not making money on some orders.

Talking to the installation teams, we realised there were issues when fitting sheds and fencing on private sites which was causing us to lose money on labour. For example, there might not be a side entrance to gain access to the garden; the ground might not be level; there might not be parking for the truck to unload; the customer might not be at the house; or an extra man would be taken on the job that wasn't allowed for.

The solution was to redesign the sales order form, listing out the above issues. The customer had to tick the boxes confirming that everything was in order. This immediately eliminated most of the problems.

Henry & Shirley posing for an Irish Times *interview.*

The building sites were harder to control. When Henry received an enquiry, the builder would send him the site map, which he would measure and thus calculate the amount of material and labour required. The price was locked in for the duration of the contract. Therefore, any material or additional labour incurred was a loss to us unless it could be used for a job outside of the contract.

We designed a system to track the panels and material being delivered to the sites, the amount of concrete being used, and the actual labour used. I input the information into a spreadsheet that Henry would tie in with his monthly invoice to the builder. Again, this highlighted costs we needed to get under control.

TIP: It's important to know how much it costs to produce your product – your materials and labour, your costs/overheads – so that you know how much you need to charge. Allow for things to go wrong – which they will. Track your performance.

As the sites were so busy, the builders had us under a lot of pressure, particularly when there was a deadline for the showhouses being opened. To keep up with the demand, we were constantly transferring installation teams from one site to another to keep everyone happy. But these teams were also trying to fit fencing and decking in private gardens, along with fitting side gates and playgrounds. It took a lot of juggling and was not cost-effective for the company! In fact, we found we were losing money in some areas.

TIP: Try not to take staff issues personally and don't get upset when things go wrong – it's part of running a business.

One of the main issues on the building sites was poor weather conditions, which would cause the ground to be too wet and mucky to work. Fortunately, in most cases, we could bring the lads back to the yard to make fence panels. This wasn't ideal as they would fall behind on the sites; however, it was better than sending them home.

Everyone in the company was trained in-house to be adaptable to work in the various departments. We had very good employee morale, together with a very high retention rate. The culture that was instilled in the company from start-up was very much alive. The *craic* and banter between staff, customers and suppliers was unreal. The lads still placed bets among themselves and with suppliers and customers for football matches and anything else they could think of! They played cards every day in the canteen.

It was unfortunate then that two of guys who had been with the company a good few years started to complain – and then things escalated.

It was our first time to appear in the Tribunal court, which we found very daunting. Although we proved there was no wrongdoing on our side and we won the case, we were instructed to pay one of them €560 and the whole thing cost the company a further €2,000 in solicitors' fees. It was all really upsetting.

The service O'Kelly's Sawmill provided from site survey, design, manufacture, and erection gave us a unique competitive advantage in the market. The company had gained a reputation for top quality products and service. So we engaged with a marketing company to set up our first website, which Henry got involved with.

In the office, it was time to move away from the manual systems as I was totally bogged down trying to keep up-to-date. We purchased the Take Five accounting package, which suited our needs and eliminated a lot of manual administration.

I was always amazed how so many companies would wait until the end of their financial year to have their accounts audited by their accountants to find out if they were making or losing money. I was able to produce our own profit and loss accounts within a few days of the month-end. This gave us great control of the finances and bank accounts – very important, because it was our own money! I designed a simple spreadsheet for daily cash flow that I swear by and use every day. From just a quick look at it, I know exactly what the bank balance will be each day; I'm not relying on the bank to keep me up-to-date.

Henry learnt from the guys installing the computer systems as he wanted a clear understanding himself of how it all operated. He never liked being totally reliant on others. We purchased a much higher quality printer with a scanner that produced our brochures which Henry designed. This was very cost-effective as we were able to quickly make changes to the brochures.

Our website, job costing systems, computerised account systems, emails, producing brochures, etc, in-house, together with drawings for customers and architects, placed us well ahead of our competitors on technology!

However, during the period 2001 to 2004, despite increasing turnover by €1 million, it became clear that our sales growth and margins were hampered by our inability to increase manufacturing output or to establish a competitive cost-base. The manufacturing processes were predominantly manual, and we were unable to recruit suitable candidates to help grow the business.

At that time, at the height of the Celtic Tiger, Ireland was at full employment. We were struggling to get workers. A lot of foreign nationals were coming to Ireland to work. We were given a contact of a concrete company which was employing some of them. They arranged for Henry to meet a guy at their premises. They warned Henry that most likely the guy would not speak English and that we would have to set him up with accommodation. Sure enough, he had no English whatsoever, not a word! But Dainis worked with us for years until he left to set up his own garage. He now services our fleet of vans.

A Sunday Times article about O'Kelly's Sawmill's international recruitment.

A few weeks later, another few lads came over to work. Henry and I went looking for accommodation for them, which was very difficult as house prices and rents were very high. We rented and furnished a house close by in Firhouse for them and set them up with bank accounts. They were trained to make fence panels and to fit fencing. The only way Henry could communicate was through sign language, drawing pictures and using matchsticks which resembled men!

They were a nice group of lads, very polite, quick learners and hungry to work. They were on a mission to make as much money as possible and working long hours wasn't a problem. This resulted in an increase in production, sales, and profits for the company.

One Sunday morning, they arrived into Henry in a panic. After some difficulty understanding them, eventually he realised they had lost one of the group – Edgar – in town the previous evening. He had no English, or phone, and hadn't a clue what his address was. The only thing Henry could think of was to phone the Gardaí. Fortunately, they had found Edgar wandering around lost and took him into shelter for the night. All turned out well!

In 2004, we had a workforce of 32 employees, who were doing their best to help grow the business. However, we needed a thorough evaluation of the business and a practical business plan to get us through the next stage of development.

Henry and I had approached Enterprise Ireland for assistance on a few occasions. In March 2004, they agreed to evaluate our business and approved us for support under the Competitiveness Improvement Program for SMEs. A critical part of the evaluation was to determine the factor(s) that would enable us to gain sustainable competitive advantage in the markets we served. A summary of the evaluation is outlined on the next page. With a background in business process re-engineering, industrial engineering and lean, Vincent Langan was appointed as our consultant. He had worked with many SMEs, enabling them to develop into sustainable and profitable enterprises.

At the outset, Vincent explained that he would be "wearing the customer's hat", identifying tasks and processes that did not add customer value. Together with the management team and employees, he would guide us in eliminating these non-added value activities. Acting as the customer's representative, Vincent had final say in what added customer value. He used a very simple criterion:

Customer value is anything for which the customer is prepared to pay.

If the customer is not prepared to pay, then it does not add value and must be eliminated. Where we do add customer value, we will try to improve the process and achieve best-in-class performance.

To emphasise the strategic message he wanted to convey, Vincent issued the following commitment:

We will make every effort to ensure that we never ask an employee, supplier or stakeholder in the business to complete any task or process, or supply any service, that we know will not add customer value.

We assured our employees that we were not seeking greater physical effort. What we wanted was their full commitment to apply their knowledge, skills, and attitude to devising and implementing best practice throughout the enterprise. Jointly identifying constraints and impediments to best practice was a key factor in Vincent's approach.

FACTORS	CURRENT STRATEGY	FUTURE STRATEGY
Innovation – Differentiation	Predominantly our range of fencing and garden sheds are standard items as per market preference.	Continue current strategy.
	We show **innovation** in our unique designs of garden furniture, playgrounds and landscape Items.	Continue current strategy.
	Differentiation is reflected in the acknowledged quality of the O'Kelly's Sawmill range of product. We use highest grade raw materials matched with the skills, knowledge, and attitude of our employees.	Continue current strategy.
Cost Leader	O'Kelly's Sawmill & The Shed Man is considered more expensive than similar products in the market. On inspection, customers find that our product is of a higher specification and finish than our competitors. We live by the motto *"quality is remembered long after price is forgotten"*.	Continue current strategy.
Customer Service	Priority of supply is given to the commercial sector, builders, and contractors. This can result in the lead time for private and domestic customers varying and is a source of disappointment to them.	Devise and implement manufacturing processes together with realistic planning and scheduling that ensures agreed lead times are maintained and all our customers receive the service level they expect and deserve.

This approach got early buy-in from the employees and ensured that they took ownership of the process. This ownership gave employees the motivation to fully participate in achieving a continuous improvement environment.

There were no accurate KPIs or performance data for manufacturing output within the company, which resulted in a lack of accountability. Consequently, it was necessary to establish time standards for each process and product category. It was agreed to undertake a programme of work measurement to cover all manufacturing processes. Vincent convinced the employees that measurement is the first step that leads to control and eventually to improvement. His key message was:

If you cannot measure something, you cannot understand it.
If you cannot understand it, you cannot control it.

If you cannot control it, you cannot improve it.

Any worries about time studies from the employees was overcome by assuring the staff that no KPI would be implemented without agreement that it was accurate, fair, and equitable. We soon had accurate output standards, together with realistic and agreed KPIs.

The initial phase of the business plan was completed by the end of 2004 and started showing real results by 2005. Sales in 2005 were 34% ahead of 2004, with net profit exceeding the business plan target by 100%, and sales turnover per employee increased by 22%. This performance was achieved with only three additional employees and no capital expenditure.

TIP: Customer value is anything for which the customer is prepared to pay. If the customer is not prepared to pay, then it does not add value and must be eliminated.

FAMILY SADNESS

In June 2004, my parents celebrated their 50th wedding anniversary in the Radisson Hotel, Dublin. With such a large family and circle of friends through motor and motorcycle sport, it was a huge gathering. Little did we know it was to be the last gathering!

Mum and Dad on their wedding day.

My Dad had a massive heart attack the following September. We were told he wouldn't survive, but he did – except he suffered a lot of damage that he never fully recovered from. He was transferred from Naas Hospital to a nursing home a few minutes from the family home.

Mum contacted friends of the family, Tony and Regina Clarke, who were funeral undertakers. She also picked out his suit and had it cleaned for him to be buried in. All just in case.

At Christmas, Dad was allowed to go home for the day. I was booked to go to Florida with Henry and the children and my sister Susan's family. We were worried about going, but Mum insisted everything would be fine. There were plenty of family at home.

On 30 December, we received a phone call in Florida from my brother Trevor to say that Mum had a massive heart attack in her sleep and was found dead that morning by my sister Hilary.

Even though Dad was not in great health, he insisted on organising Mum's funeral. He picked out the dress he wanted her buried in and made the arrangements with the undertaker. I will never forget seeing him struggle to walk up the aisle in the church, heart-broken.

He returned to the nursing home; the family took turns in bringing him home for a few hours, but he had no will to live. He died the following April of a broken heart. The family didn't have to arrange the funeral, as Mum had already done it. It was bizarre the way they both arranged one another's funerals. We all knew one was never going to live long without the other as they were such a united couple and spent all their days together.

So, within a year of the celebrations in the Radisson, they were both buried in Eadestown, Co Kildare.

TIMBERTROVE

TIMBERTROVE GETS ITS NAME

Henry and I decided to enter the SFA National Small Business Awards 2005. This entailed a detailed submission under a range of headings, which was a great opportunity to re-evaluate the business, reflecting on our achievements and setting out our plans for the future.

We were delighted to be shortlisted as Finalists in the two categories we had entered: Manufacturing and Retail. We were one of 34 companies shortlisted across six categories.

The awards presentation took place at a Gala Awards Banquet held in the Berkeley Court Hotel and the awards were presented by the Patron of the Awards, An Taoiseach, Bertie Ahern TD. Video footage of the finalists at their premises was shown on the night. Finalists also featured in a full colour supplement in the *Irish Independent*, which gave us great exposure.

The finalists had been announced a few weeks earlier at a Gala Reception in the House of Lords, in College Green, Dublin, where the guest speaker for the evening was Liam Birkett, an intellectual property and business development consultant.

We always have been conscious of the importance of our brand. We always tried to improve our brochures, website, and overall appearance of our premises. The last could be quite challenging at times – a timber yard up the mountains creates a lot of dirt, particularly in the wintertime. But we like to think that customers are proud of having our product in their gardens with the company badge on it. So we were delighted when we met Liam. He was exactly what we needed to enhance our brand. We knew O'Kelly's Sawmill and The Shed Man names were limiting us, as they didn't describe the business very well. Liam's first suggestion was to rebrand to Timbertrove and he added a tagline:

Wood products you will treasure for life.

Henry and I both immediately fell in love with the new brand!

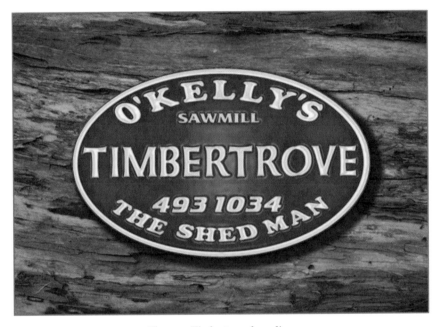

The new Timbertrove branding.

After several visits, Liam compiled a list of suggestions to renovate the premises, showrooms and website to improve the brand awareness before launching the new brand. For example, the showrooms carried a vast range of DIY, tools, paints, garden supplies, clothing and giftware to increase the customer spend. Major improvements were made to the display of products by identifying them with appealing names, sales messages, and price tags. Improvements also were made to our brochures and website with the new brand. Signage was replaced around the premises, making it more attractive for the customer to visit.

Commercial Feature

Timbertrove – proud of its new image but in no hurry to shed original branding

A LOCAL timber company, known by most as O'Kelly's ('The Shed Man'), has been crowned the manufacturing category winners' in the coveted SFA National Small Business Awards 2006.

For a quarter of a century O'Kelly's, now known as Timbertrove, has nestled at the foot of the Dublin mountains just below the Hellfire Club in Killakee, creating "wood products you will treasure for life".

Over the years the company has undergone many transformational changes and has now metamorphosed into its ultimate identity, Timbertrove.

However, recognising that the O'Kelly name has served them well over the years, this familiar emblem still lives on in the company's branding.

Timbertrove's wood products are manufactured to the highest of standards and "nothing is spared to ensure that customer satisfaction is assured".

Their range of products is in constant development so as to cater for the diverse requirements of designers, architects and builders, as well as new trends in the wider consumer market.

The company has also designed, manufactured and erected creative and robust designs for Dublin Zoo and Fota Wildlife Park thus providing commercial customers with a "one-stop-shop" facility.

So, as the bright summer days begin to lighten up our lives, and our back gardens, why not pay Timbertrove a visit and view their extensive display of products, such as tree-houses, play-units, fencing, sheds, timber decks, garden furniture, gazebos, pergola, trellis and side gates... all of which carry the Timbertrove Guarantee.

SAVE €25.00 Swing Sets in kit form were €215 now only €190 plus a choice of swing accessories FREE

Fencing - Treehouses - Playunits - Sheds
Timber Decks - Garden Furniture
Gazebo - Pergola - Trellis - Bridges
Dog Kennels - Side Gates made to order
Noise Barrier - Soil Retaining
Playgrounds as seen in
Dublin Zoo, Fota Wildlife Park,
Bunratty Castle & Folk Park

493 1034

Fax 493 4406
KILLAKEE, RATHFARNHAM, DUBLIN 16
Opp. Hellfire Club
www .timbertrove.com

An article in the Echo about our rebranding.

A five-year guarantee was offered on our garden sheds and the following sign was displayed prominently:

Top 10 reasons to deal with Timbertrove

❖ We believe our success is based on differentiation through innovative design, quality materials and craftsmanship in addition to superior customer service.

❖ 20 years' experience, family business with a very experienced dedicated workforce.

❖ Buy direct from the source. Products can be custom-made.

❖ Free advice from the experts you can trust.

❖ One stop shop: DIY store, drive-in fuel depot, giftware and much more.

❖ Full installation and delivery service. Fully insured.

❖ Products carry the Timbertrove guarantee.

❖ Support local Irish business.

❖ Visit our showrooms situated in the Dublin Mountains, just below the Hellfire Club with spectacular views overlooking Dublin Bay.

❖ Buy online.

It's no secret we're the best in town!

Later in the year, Linda, my niece, joined the company to help with the administration in the sales office, working part-time while studying in college. She was a breath of fresh air! The first female to join the business and it was no bother to her working with the lads – she was well able for them!

Henry with our newly-rebranded truck.

ONWARDS & UPWARDS

One of the keys to Timbertrove's success has been the flexibility in our manufacturing to meet customer specifications and service levels. This flexibility has been achieved, in the main, through mostly manual and labour-intensive processes. We wanted to maintain this flexibility while, at the same time, optimising output and efficiency.

We formed task teams for each product category, and these task teams were given the formal training and responsibility for devising and implementing best practice procedures for maximising productivity throughout the Timbertrove supply chain from design, procurement, manufacturing right through to erection on site.

Timbertrove trellis and fencing on display at the RDS.

The workings of the task teams were based on employees:

- Knowing what managers know.
- Understanding the challenges facing the company and the plans to deal with them.
- Developing the skills that allow them to take part in participative activities, including speaking up in front of others, confronting differences, understanding how to reach consensus, facilitating the participation of others, and listening.

Our employees embraced change and they now play a constructive role in maintaining a continuous improvement environment. We are customer-focused, in that every one of our employees strive to deliver the service and added value our customers expect and deserve.

In 2006, we measured our productivity based on sales turnover per employee. The performance was outstanding; we achieved a 34% increase in turnover per employee, without any additional capital investment. The increase was the result of better methods and procedures, leadership, and the commitment of a motivated workforce.

> **TIP: Never be afraid of change; keep looking for new ideas. We constantly strive to improve, adapt, and add to our product range.**

Henry and I were so delighted with the developments and improvements in the performance of the business from 2005 to 2006 that we entered the SFA National Small Business Awards 2006, determined to win this time. And we did! We were outright winners of the Manufacturing category. This was a great achievement for the company. We received tremendous publicity and celebrated by taking the employees with their partners to an overnight stay in a hotel in Kilkenny with the cash prize of €5,000.

187

O'Kelly Sawmills & The Shed Man

Address: Killakee, Rathfarnham, Dublin 16.
Tel: 01 493 1034 **Fax:** 01 493 4412
Website: www.timbertrove.com
Year End: 31/08/05
Main Activities/Speciality Work:
Manufacture and installer of timber fencing, garden sheds, playground equipment and supplier of all types of timber and fence panels
Executives: Chief Executive: Henry O'Kelly; Director Shirley O'Kelly
No. of Employees: 35

Turnover: €3,600,000

#187 among construction companies in Ireland!

O'Kelly Sawmills won the Manufacturing category. Pictured were Frank Ryan, CEO, Enterprise Ireland with Shirley and Henry O'Kelly, O'Kelly Sawmills

We won! Manufacturing category winner, SFA National Small Business Awards, 2006.

A few months later, I was invited to be a guest speaker at the launch of the next year's awards in the Guinness Storehouse. I recall being extremely nervous, it being my first time to speak in public. Pat Delaney, then the Director of the SFA, said, "Just tell your story from the heart". That's what I did, and it got the audience laughing a few times! Pat's advice has always stayed with me, and this book is based on it.

We were supplying and fitting a lot of timber decking, which got very slippy when it was wet and required a lot of maintenance. Henry had been researching an alternative. He attended a builders' exhibition in America where he came across composite decking. It was low maintenance, slip-resistant and lasted much longer than timber decking. The boards were easily clipped together and came in various colours, making it very attractive. Decorative handrail and posts were available to match the decking.

Although it was more expensive, Henry was confident that it would be a good seller – particularly with the builders.

We applied to be appointed the sole distributor in Ireland for the decking. One of the American company's representatives visited our premises and was very impressed. After lengthy discussions, Timbertrove was appointed the sole distributor in Ireland for Latitude Composite Decking. At the time, this type of decking was not available in Ireland – so once again, Timbertrove was ahead of the competition!

Our first container of decking boards, handrails and posts, all in various colours, took eight weeks to transport from America – and had to be paid for in full before despatch. In the meantime, we arranged to get samples, which Henry gave to the builders to secure some orders for when the container arrived. Fortunately, one builder was starting a new site and decided to try the composite decking as opposed to timber. This decision quickly was followed with orders from other builders.

We also built and displayed a small deck in our showrooms, which drew a lot of interest and generated orders to supply and fit this new type of decking in customers' gardens.

In 2007, I recall thinking, "Things just couldn't get any better". Business was good: we had 48 employees and almost €4m in turnover. Cashflow was strong. We had invested the profits in improvements to our premises, a fleet of trucks together with machines, equipment and computerised systems. Twenty-one years on, we had come a long way from the hayshed and Amy, the old red tractor!

To our surprise, our next-door neighbours informed us that they were putting their house on the market. Henry had helped to build this house, which he had lived in with his family until they sold it. It made commercial sense to buy it as the sawmill had outgrown the yard it was situated on. The bank was quite happy to sanction a loan, particularly as the business was in such a strong position. We had changed banks a few years earlier!

I had fulfilled another dream with a new Range Rover, built to my own specifications, and Henry had fulfilled one of his dreams by purchasing a helicopter along with three friends.

Henry piloting his helicopter – with an able navigator!　　　　*Danielle and Ciara – flying!*

But, in November 2007, one of our biggest customers informed us they were going to stop building houses in the New Year. This was the first sign of slowdown and the recession that was to come in 2008!

RECESSION!

In 2008, suddenly, Ireland was in recession. For us in Timbertrove, it was like the lights were switched off overnight!

The construction industry came to a grinding halt, leaving us very little site work. The trade accounts also plummeted. It was just unbelievable how things turned so quickly!

Henry and I were quite active in networking and attended a lot of conferences where economists were saying there would be a "soft landing". The newspapers and media generally were saying the same thing.

Henry is very much an optimistic person. He kept reassuring the employees there would be a gradual slow-down and that all would be fine. But it was hard for Henry to convince me as I was looking at things from the financial side of the business. I was very worried as I was lodging less and less money in the bank every day. Regardless, the wages had to be paid to our employees each week, along with a lot of direct debits on finances, insurance and various other overheads.

Fortunately, 10 of the guys, who were from Latvia and went home for Christmas, didn't return as we had told them we couldn't guarantee work in January.

My main concern was that there was almost €750,000 owed to us from builders and trade accounts. As the company owed a similar amount to our suppliers, bank and Revenue Commissioners, we could not afford to get stung with any bad debts. My priority became collecting the money owed. Obviously, this was very difficult; however, I had built up good relationships with most customers over the years and they were well used to my persistency! I had to agree instalment payments with some of them, just to get the money in.

It was very worrying, as so many companies were going out of business at the time. Some of the companies started to bounce cheques and even cash sale customers over the counter were doing the same. But it was difficult not to take the cheques as we needed the business.

For the first three months of the year, we would normally be heavily reliant on the builders and trade accounts. The business from the domestic market would normally start late March and run through to the end of September.

Unfortunately, a few months later, we had to make the tough decision to place our employees on a three-day week. Even though most of them understood, it was absolutely heartbreaking – the toughest decision Henry and I had to make in business.

The work just wasn't there nor the money; it was getting harder every week to pay the wages. We were reluctant to entertain redundancies as we had a very good team who we had invested in training over the years and they would be hard to replace. We trusted and respected our employees who had built the business with us over the past 22 years. We knew that most of them had young children and were reliant on their wages.

SANTA'S RETURN

So, we decided to bring Santa back! The event had been such a success when it was run in the 1990s that it was worth a try! We kept costs to a minimum by doing most of the work ourselves, except for the electrical work.

Santa's back!

The flyer we circulated to advertise Santa's return to the sawmill.

Jimmy, elder brother to Adrian, John and Con who had worked in the business from the very early years, was an electrician and had done most of the electrical work in the sawmill over the years. He did the work needed for the Santa event – and didn't charge for it, knowing the pressure we were under. He said to Henry, "Just try and keep the brothers in a job!" It was such a kind gesture – we'll never forget it!

I invested in good quality costumes which I sourced in America for Santa, Mrs. Claus and her helper in the kitchen. I also purchased elves costumes with the tights and shoes which were cool! I sourced a toy supplier for the individual presents in Santa bags, splitting them between boys and girls and across three different age groups.

We built Santa's room with the chimney where the elf would drop the present down, Santa's bedroom along with his workshop that the elf worked in and the kitchen. Outside, we had Santa's sleigh which the parents took photos of the children in, as well as lights and more reindeers in the trees and traditional Christmas music playing.

We set up a pre-booking system which meant we could control the numbers safely; it also told us how many presents we would require between boy / girl and age groups and how much mulled wine, mince pies and sweets we would need for the parents and children.

Our four Santas were mostly employees – even Jimmy the electrician got roped into being a Santa. Henry's Mum and Marlyn, our neighbour, shared being Mrs. Claus and the helper in kitchen. Danielle and Ciara's friends and some of the employees' children played the elves.

As soon as we announced that Santa at the Sawmill was back, bookings started to flow in – with payment, which was great for cashflow.

Sadly, our lovely Santa sign which we erected on the main road to advertise the event was nicked. But, again, we turned a negative into a positive by getting free advertising on the back of the theft!

The event was very successful and brought a welcome buzz about the place. I think people were delighted to visit the Dublin mountains and get away from the doom and gloom of the recession. Although people were not interested in placing orders for timber products, as it was a family day out, we displayed our products to thousands of potential customers and hoped that they would return in the New Year and place orders. In the meantime, we sold giftware, coal, firewood, Christmas logs and wreaths at the event and generated some extra income.

WORKING THROUGH THE RECESSION

After a very tough and stressful year, Timbertrove survived 2008 despite a 21% drop in sales on the previous year and a significant loss. The business closed for the Christmas / New Year period. Everyone was paid and went home to enjoy their holidays.

For Henry and myself, being married and living beside the business with three children, there was constant pressure 24 / 7 trying to think up new ideas. I can recall how terrifying and depressing it was to see everything fall apart so quickly. It was like being in a dark tunnel with no light in sight! There was a lot of conflict between us trying to agree and make the right decisions for the business. It required both our expertise to fight the recession and survive.

The thought crossed our minds whether we should just lock the gates and walk away before we lost any more money. But Timbertrove had a very good reputation with its customers and suppliers and neither Henry nor I could walk away and leave them stuck for money. We had never defaulted on payment nor ever bounced a cheque, and we weren't prepared to start now. We kept reminding ourselves why we started the business in the first place.

We had no idea how long the recession was going to last but we knew we had to keep fighting for what we had worked so hard for. We were very proud of the successful business we had built. Even though I was terrified, there was a voice in the back of my head saying, "You can do this".

So we headed into 2009, still in the dark tunnel with no light in sight!

TIP: Have a rainy-day bank account on reserve.

When we returned to work in 2009, we got hassle from a small group of employees, who insisted on wanting to know when they would return to full-time employment.

We held several meetings with the group and Henry explained the situation the company was in. They could see for themselves that they were struggling to fill their day with work and that the yard had very little stock. However, they refused to cooperate; they didn't want to know the company's problems, they were only interested in their own. It was very stressful and disappointing as we had always looked after the employees as best we could.

Eventually, the group decided to take statutory redundancy.

Thankfully, there was some activity on the building sites – supplying timber and panels to civil engineering companies and landscapers – not a lot, but every job helped to keep the wheels turning. Some of the main timber suppliers started to buy panels from us, which helped at the end of the month since we could exchange payments.

The payroll had been reduced; however, we were still under pressure to reduce the overheads, although some of them – like insurance and utilities – were out of our control.

Henry was optimistic that things would improve in April with the domestic market. We soon found out this was not the case; timber products were not a priority on the household to do list. Our sales figures were dropping at an enormous rate, month after month, leading to losses.

Several years earlier, when we had financed one of our first trucks, the repayments were just over €500 per month. When the loan was cleared off, Henry cleverly suggested we open a deposit account and continue paying the money into it for a rainy day! Over the years, any spare money we had was transferred into this deposit account and it had built up into a substantial amount of money. We were under enormous financial pressure trying to keep the bank account within its overdraft limit and, in addition, we were falling behind with suppliers and the Revenue Commissioners. So we started to transfer money from the rainy-day deposit account until it ran out.

W e had heard that "Bloom in the Park" was a very popular event, targeted specifically at garden lovers. We booked a stand for the 2009 event, and made up some sheds, fencing, and other products from the range to display to secure orders.

Danielle manning the Timbertrove stand at Bloom in the Park.

Latitude decking on display at the Bloom in the Park garden show.

Henry and I, with Linda and our children, Danielle, Ciara, and Conor (then 17, 14 and 12), handed out brochures with special limited time offers and an invite to follow us on Facebook.

Our stand was situated in a very prominent area close to the show gardens. We attracted a lot of people onto the stand who hadn't heard of Timbertrove before. We displayed the Latitude slip-resistant decking, which proved to be popular. We didn't generate many orders even with the special offers, but it kept the wheels turning! And, following the event, new customers visited the showrooms so, overall, we felt it was a great success.

When we submitted our audited accounts for the financial year ending 31 August 2008 to the bank, we received a letter expressing the bank's disappointment with the loss the company had made. However, the bank was keen to support us in the difficult trading environment, but wanted an in-depth analysis of the viability of the company to allow them to continue supporting the business. Not an unreasonable request!

With our accountants, we prepared the following for the next year:

- Management accounts.
- Cash flow projections.
- Detailed proposals to turn the company around from lossmaking to profit.
- Proposed cost-cutting measures.
- Statement of affairs.

Our proposal to the bank to turn the company around started by giving them a little insight into our upbringing, how we started the business and the success it had been until we were struck totally out of the blue with a worldwide recession.

To get back to making profit, we proposed:

- Extending Saturday opening hours to 4pm and opening on Sundays from 2pm to 5pm. Henry and I, with our three children, would run the operation so no additional wages would be incurred.

- Expanding the range of showroom merchandise, which included giftware, garden accessories, DIY, pet zone and clothing, working with suppliers on a sale-or-return basis.
- Setting up a drive-in fuel depot selling coal, briquettes and logs.
- Installing a push-button coffee machine, along with confectionery and drinks.
- Designing and manufacturing a "recession-affordable" range of garden furniture and sheds.
- The return of Santa at Christmas.

With the recession, there was an increase in traffic at the weekends with people visiting the Dublin mountains and going for walks to the Hellfire Club and Massy's Wood adjacent to us. It was cheaper to take the children for a walk than going to the movies.

Quickly, the turnaround plan submitted to the bank started to take effect. People were browsing around the showrooms at the weekends, buying little bits and pieces and having a cup of coffee. The coal, briquettes and logs also sold well.

Typically during the week, one partner in a couple would call in to look at a shed or fencing; in a lot of cases, they would have to get the other partner to have a look before placing the order. With the extended weekend hours, both partners were able to come in and nine out of 10 times they would place an order.

I would be in the office late on Saturday and Sunday evenings, trying to set up the new customers on the computer and process their orders and payments that Henry had taken. Henry's expertise really was in capturing the order with the customers – he was very good at this! He closed lots of sales. He was very witty with the customers and had a great personality. One of our key selling points was the great knowledge of timber products that Henry and the guys had and their ability to advise customers.

The Santa event was run over a few weekends in December, again attracting thousands with the pre-booking system and payments upfront. Even though running the event was extremely hard work, there was a great buzz about the place. Everyone was happy, and you could almost forget there was a recession.

Christmas was tough financially, being closed for almost two weeks with no sales and paying out the wages. My sister Susan kindly offered to lend us money from her redundancy to pay the wages over Christmas; we repaid her in January.

Despite a further drop in sales of 46% on the previous year, we reduced overheads and so reduced losses on the previous year.

By 2010, Timbertrove was down to 13 employees, plus Henry and myself. The pressure continued to mount as I tried to juggle the finances. Waking up in the morning, I would lift my head off the pillow – it felt like it weighed a ton! Next, I would wrap my hands around one leg to lift it to the side of the bed, followed by the other. Then I would sit for a few minutes thinking of who would be phoning today looking for money and who I had promised to phone with an update of payments. I knew the first email would be from the bank, detailing what direct debits were going through that day and wanting to know how much I was going to lodge. My cashflow gave me this information, so the email was never a surprise. I would normally go to the bank a couple of times a week; now I was going every day. As soon as money came in, it was banked – some days, the lodgement was only a couple of hundred euros.

A Sunday Times article from 2009 and an interview in The Star in 2008.

Most of our suppliers had placed our accounts on hold. Henry got to the stage where he literally had no timber in the yard. When we received an order for a shed, he would have to go to the local building providers to buy timber and pay for it. Then he had to go to Churchtown Stores Hardware and buy a roll of felt for the roof, paying the same retail price as the customer would – no trade discount. It was total madness, more expensive plus the cost of the driver and truck. But it was what we had to do to keep the wheels turning.

One day, a representative from the Revenue Commissioners arrived at the office. In fairness, he was very understanding. I explained we were not trying to default, just trying to survive; the Revenue would get paid as soon as we had the money. We agreed an instalment payment plan; unfortunately, we had to pay interest. The other main issue was the Revenue wouldn't issue a tax clearance certificate, which we needed for the local councils that we had been supplying timber to over the past 20 years. We were also paying a lot of interest to the bank, as our overdraft facility was constantly on the limit.

Danielle, Ciara and Conor on our stand at Bloom, 2010.

For Bloom 2010, we decided we had to generate more sales. We took stock from the showrooms and set up a shop alongside the timber products stand to sell garden accessories, giftware, and clothing. Danielle, Ciara and Conor said they would run the shop if they were paid a commission! Well-trained children! They were 18, 15 and 13 years old at the time. Henry and I manned the timber stand to save wages. Conor had bought a small machine to chop logs a few years earlier. He sold the logs at the show, although he made the money for himself!

It was really hard work building the stand, loading and unloading the merchandise. Most companies had marquees they zipped up when the show was finished at 6pm. We hadn't that luxury, so we had to pack everything away and set again up each morning for five days. It was torture! But the giftware attracted more people onto the stand. Thankfully, we had sourced unusual garden accessories with price points of under €10 and €20, which sold very well. We achieved sales orders for the timber products, along with the sales of the giftware shop – less the commission for the children! Mission accomplished, I happily went to the bank with a lodgement that paid off another few bills!

The orders from Bloom kept us going for a few months, along with orders received afterwards. The Santa event took place in December and, yet again, was a success. But every day was spent juggling the finances and trying to come up with new ideas. Henry's days were spent trying to drum up business to keep the lads busy and cover the payroll.

At the end of 2010, after all our hard work, there was a further 10% drop in sales against the previous year – but again, we had managed to reduce the loss slightly. While this was an improvement, we were still under fierce pressure for money.

We were both worn out. We had injected most of our savings into the business; we had cut our own wages; we had no heating oil for the house, though fortunately we had offcuts of timber to burn on the fire! We had come through 2008, 2009 and 2010, three terrifying and stressful years, losing money. It was soul-destroying and heart-breaking. While both families were concerned and asked from time to time how we were doing, they couldn't fully understand the stress and fear we were carrying every day. The only bit of comfort we got was from talking to people from other companies that were also struggling – and there was a lot of them, some which unfortunately didn't survive.

So we tried to switch off over Christmas; we badly needed to recharge the batteries!

FIGHTING BACK

Starting 2011, Henry and I were on a mission to increase sales. We knew we also needed to work more efficiently to reduce labour and diesel costs; and we needed to buy timber at the right price to increase margins and hopefully make a profit rather than a loss. We really had no control over the other overheads we were carrying.

We still had 13 employees, most of them with the company from the beginning. They were very adaptable; they could be making sheds in the morning and fitting in the afternoon, then making fence panels another day or out on-site erecting and later making garden furniture. They were still on a three-day week; however, if we received orders that couldn't be completed within this time, the staff would work extra hours for free just to get the orders out and get paid. They were just great!

Henry and I were trying to restructure our loan facilities with the bank. A colleague who ran a large business recommended a consultant who had over 20 years' experience in banking before setting up his own business specialising in business turnaround. Perhaps he would have the solutions to all our problems!

It was the first time we had an independent person to talk to. At our first meeting with him, John asked two questions:

- Was it a good idea in the first place to set up the business?
- Have you the balls to keep going?

Without any hesitation, we both said "Yes" to both questions.

Over several meetings that went on late into the evenings, we went through the history of the business, where we had come from, where we were at and where we wanted to be. We got on very well with John, so we hired him to take over negotiations with the bank and to free me up to concentrate on running the business.

When a new bank manager was appointed, he came to the sawmill to introduce himself. A very nice man – but his parting words were: "I hope we can have a good relationship but don't come to me with the next set of accounts showing a loss!" This was at the height of a recession when the banks themselves were losing a fortune!

Sales remained pretty much on par with the previous year. There was some activity with the builders and landscapers. A couple of guys who had worked for us had set up their own business erecting fencing. In fairness, they bought their panels from Timbertrove, which was a great help. The shed sales just about ticked over.

When we looked back on our photos from Bloom the previous year, we realised the stand was very cluttered with giftware and that we hadn't showcased the timber products very well.

Henry had an old trailer on which he built a shop, which we put at one side of the stand. We decorated the timber products with some of the giftware. And with our experience from the previous year, we had a better idea of what would sell. In 2011, metal table and chair sets, metal arch and metal planters, vegetable trugs, seeds, cast iron door knockers, bells and decorative hooks for the sheds all sold out. Decorative bits, mostly under €10, flew out the door. Everything was under €20; we had learnt that was the price point. The other thing we had learnt was that people would only buy things that weren't too heavy or awkward to carry.

I used to love the Thursday and Friday at the show. Women would come in groups; there were bus loads from the North and South on a day out to spend money. They were all dressed up for Bloom and in top form.

Saturday, Sunday, and the bank holiday Monday were different. Most people those days came as couples – and some of the men would be saying, "Do you really need that?" Not helpful! On the upside, there were more children at the weekends, so the garden tools, clothing and small decorative things sold to them.

In selling mode at Bloom.

Overall, this year, there was more interest in the timber products; we secured more orders at the show, probably due to better display.

But there was a lot of preparation: sourcing and buying the giftware, loading and unloading for the five-day event, packing everything away every night into the trailer and unloading again every morning. The timber products had to be manufactured, transported, and erected in Bloom – and then taken down the day after the show. We gained a reputation at Bloom with the organisers and security guys: Timbertrove was always first in and last out!

Despite the hard work, it's a great event. We realised it was great for PR. A lot of customers came onto the stand to say they had bought their shed or fencing from us and were delighted with the quality and service, which was encouraging for us to hear when we were under such pressure.

We also met builders and landscaper customers, along with some of our suppliers; we even met our bank manager! At least he saw us and the children trying. But I remember introducing Conor to him and afterwards I said to Conor, "Someday, you'll be opening a bank account with him". His reply was classic: "I'm not giving him my money".

And after the show, with a smile on my face, I went to the bank with my lodgement which paid another few bills!

We had been told by a cousin of Henry's that the Tullamore Show would be worth exhibiting at. It was held in August. As we had the shop on the trailer, we decided to exhibit.

Our shop at the Tullamore Show, August 2011 – on the trailer that Henry built!

Again, we loaded up with giftware and brochures on the timber products. The traffic was horrendous. Eventually, we arrived at our spot which was stuck up the back, out of the way. The few customers who stopped at our stand just looked and walked away. We tried to give out brochures and get their email address to add to our database; they hadn't heard of email. We tried for mobile numbers and most hadn't got one! An absolute disaster!

The following month was the Ploughing Championships, a huge event held over three days. We decided to exhibit.

Again, Henry and I, with Danielle, Ciara and Conor, loaded up each morning with our giftware and some timber products and battled our way through the traffic to get to our stand, unload and display the giftware for sale.

From the beginning, we were up to our knees in muck. Again, few email addresses or mobile numbers – not even with a swing as a prize. And people walked around the giftware with their hands in their pockets saying, "That's an awful price". Another disaster. We decided no more Tullamore or Ploughing events for us.

Our third try was the Enniskerry Victorian Field Day, held in September. The organisers contacted Henry to sponsor them with a shed which we agreed. As it was local, we thought it would be good advertising and hopefully bring in some orders.

We set up a giftshop, which went reasonably well. We also gave out brochures and were more successful in getting mobile numbers and email addresses to add to our database.

It was suggested that we should run an event at Halloween, linking it to the Santa event. The theme was that one of Santa's elves had been captured, and had to be released to help Santa for Christmas. The only way to do this was if the children learned how to make a special potion, wave a magic wand and shout out the magic spell (which just happened to be "Timbertrove"!).

The trail was set out. When the children arrived, they were greeted by the Head Witch – one of Ciara's friends who had studied drama – who gave each child a magic wand. She explained they had to go into each shed and help the other witches make the potion. As a result, we had hundreds of children running around having great fun, shouting out "Timbertrove". Hopefully, they'll be future customers! A percentage of the proceeds went to Laura Lynn Foundation.

John ('Locky') multi-tasking at our Halloween event.

The Santa event was even more magical this year, because it snowed. Although the roads were blocked in places with several feet of snow, the lads kept the carpark clear and safe.

I became a member of Going for Growth, a support programme for women who are serious about growing their business. The initiative is based on interactive roundtable sessions facilitated by successful entrepreneurs. It is funded by Enterprise Ireland and KPMG. The lead entrepreneurs have practical knowledge with first-hand experience of owning and managing a business that has achieved considerable growth.

I found the programme invaluable. I realised most of the other women were in a similar situation and experiencing similar problems in running their own business. It was great to be able to sit and discuss your issues and learn from each other in an environment that was totally confidential.

A magical winter wonderland welcoming Santa to Timbertrove.

Despite all our efforts, we finished the year with a further drop of 12% in sales against the previous year; although we reduced the loss, we didn't make a profit which we had hoped for. I recall feeling that I was in a dark place, totally run down, having gone through 2008, 2009, 2010 and 2011 losing money. Enormous pressure between myself and Henry, completely unable to get away from the business and its problems.

Henry recalls those few years as the worst time of his life. He was totally physically and mentally exhausted. It was so hard getting out of bed every morning to go to work and lose money. If he had known the recession was going to get so bad, he would have paid off the suppliers, bank and Revenue, paid redundancies and closed the gates and sat tight until things improved. We would have been much better off. But we were so emotionally attached to the company, employees, and their families. It was soul-destroying not having any money and losing so much of what we had worked hard for.

Henry also found it very difficult and upsetting watching some companies file for insolvency in the UK and being cleared two years later, as well as companies that were liquidated or just closed and started again under another name with a clear slate. We absolutely struggled so much to pay everyone we owed money to.

We knew we needed to get away from the business. So we decided to go to our house in Florida, which had been rented out since we purchased it to cover the costs.

At the Going for Growth conference in Barberstown Castle, I had met a lady, who was in a similar situation with her business. She said she had read a book called *Flourishing* by Maureen Gaffney, which she had found very helpful. The subtitle of the book was *How to achieve a deeper sense of well-being, meaning and purpose – even when facing adversity.* This really spoke to me!

I read the book, along with some others written by successful entrepreneurs. I was seeking inspiration. And then one day it occurred to me that I couldn't give the bank, suppliers or Revenue what I didn't have: money! All the sleepless nights and worrying I was doing wasn't solving the problems. I had to come up with something different for 2012.

A CHANGE OF FOCUS

We returned to work in January feeling refreshed, motivated, and positive! We stopped watching the news and reading the newspapers. We stopped listening to negative talk.

I arranged individual meetings with our main suppliers. I explained the situation, how hard we had had fought over the past four years and how we were going to continue fighting. My proposal was that they supply us with a cash on delivery basis and whatever extra money we had, we would pay off the account – or else we'd close the gates, liquidate the company and they would get nothing!

It was a no brainer for them! The suppliers were also suffering in the recession. This way, they got to sell timber, were paid C.O.D. and the balance on the account was being reduced.

They all agreed – except for two, who closed our accounts and put us under enormous pressure to pay the outstanding balances.

But, overall, the arrangement meant Timbertrove was back buying timber at sensible prices – far cheaper than buying as we needed it from local builders providers. Better still, most of our orders were now being delivered to the yard, saving us labour and diesel.

We had built up good relationships with most of the suppliers over the years. They knew we had a great team of workers and that Timbertrove was number one in the business of supplying top quality sheds and fencing. They also could see we were open seven days a week with a retail showroom, as well as participating in exhibitions and holding events held at our premises. I promised that when the recession passed, and our business increased, we would give them the business. That's exactly what we did – and continue to do still. We will never forget the support our suppliers gave us.

I agreed a payment plan with the Council for the rates and continued the instalment arrangement with the Revenue Commissioners.

Danielle helping to clear the snow!

Unfortunately, the snow – which had added to the atmosphere for Santa at the Sawmill in November / December – continued for most of the next few months. So the sawmill was open and closed, depending on whether the road was passable. We lost almost €150,000 in sales through to March – a setback we weren't prepared for! There was absolutely nothing we could do except watch the snow fall and the bills fall behind again!

John continued to negotiate with the bank. At one meeting, we were informed that we were being referred to the Global Restructuring Board, which specialised in helping businesses in difficulty. I recall feeling like the blood was being drained from my body; I almost passed out – and the bank manager sitting opposite knew it. I was terrified but, after the meeting, John reassured me this was a good thing; these guys would be more experienced, and their job was to help companies in difficulty.

A few months later, a meeting was set up in the bank's head office. We were met by a very nice young guy half our age, who we thought was showing us to the office to meet a team of senior officials. This was not the case. I remember thinking, "What can this guy know about running a business, yet alone turning around one in difficulty?" He said the bank wanted to appoint a company that specialised in corporate recovery, insolvency and liquidations to carry out an independent review of the business. We replied that we couldn't afford it, but were told the bank would be paying.

Part of the plan that we had agreed was that we would focus on the consumer market (B2C) by running events to attract more potential customers to our retail showrooms, which would then give the sales guys an opportunity to sell our timber products. We had a great range of DIY tools and accessories, giftware, garden products, clothing along with the drive-in fuel depot, together with our range of timber, fence panels, sheds, furniture, decking, dog kennels, potting tables, and playground equipment. And I had recently completed a course in Visual Merchandising & Display to improve the look of the showrooms.

An article in the Small Firms Association's Better Business magazine in 2012.

So we ran an Easter event with an Easter Hunt. Some of Danielle's friends dressed up as different characters and Ciara made a timber cut-out, painted with the Timbertrove logo, for the children to take photos.

Ciara painting the Easter cut-out, for children to take photos.

OUR COUNTRY CAFÉ

I had been saying for several years that we should open a café. At nearly every meeting with John and Henry, I'd say it. Neither would support the idea. Henry reckoned we wouldn't make money out of selling coffee and, if we did it, would take a few years. I think he was looking at the sales from the push-button coffee machine and chocolate bars we had set up a few years earlier.

At the Going for Growth conference in Barberstown Castle, I met Amanda Pratt of Avoca and asked her what she thought of opening a café in the Dublin mountains in a sawmill. Her response was, "What are you waiting for? Put in a few tables and chairs, buy second-hand equipment, serve good food and coffee, and see what happens". That made my mind up. I was going to do it!

I persuaded Henry (after a lot of arguing) to give me the stores department to convert into a small café, although he said, "You won't make money until at least February 2014". I kept a note of this date, reckoning I had 17 months to prove him wrong.

The lads in the sawmill thought I was pure crazy; they reckoned this was going to finish the company off. To be fair to them, because we lived beside the sawmill, they knew how undomesticated I was and how I much preferred to be in the office working. Despite an honour in domestic science in my Junior Cert (my only honour), I only cooked because I had to feed Henry and the three children. I was dreadful for putting the dinner on and going back into the office; next thing the smoke alarm would go off! So the joke in the sawmill was "Shirley's cooking".

My family also thought I was crazy; obviously, they knew me very well. When we were growing up, we all had our chores: mine was the ironing for all 13 of us; cooking and baking was not my strong point!

The independent review of the business for the bank had concluded "the company is insolvent and not viable in the short to medium term. However, if the cashflow issues could be restructured, it could operate within its facilities". The bank didn't support the idea opening a café either: they said I was "under the illusion I could open an Avoca-type of café in the Dublin Mountains and make money".

None of this stopped me; it only made me more determined to prove them and everyone else wrong. I had carried out a SWOT analysis, listing our strengths, weaknesses, opportunities and threats. My main concern was staff: I didn't plan on making coffee, baking, and serving customers myself. Simply, I needed to work on developing the business rather than being caught up in the day-to-day operations.

I felt this was our last shot at trying something new. We deserved a break after all we had been through. Scary and all as it was, I thought I could make a success of it. So, at Bloom that year, we advertised "Café opening soon at Timbertrove". Most people said they would come up to try it.

John had come up with the idea of storage solutions, so Henry designed a Tidy Tim – about the size of a wardrobe – for Bloom. It was targeted at customers who hadn't much space in the garden and couldn't afford a full-size shed. We displayed a His and Hers Tidy Tim; hers was fitted out with washing powders, household cleaners, saucepans, iron and board, soft drinks, while His stored garden tools and products, hose and tool bags. The Tidy Tims were also sold flat-pack, so no installation.

Henry designed a bike shed and a kids playshop and playhouse. We sold potting tables and vegetable trugs, as well as sheds, fencing, furniture, and dog kennels. Henry had also designed a chicken coop, which he thought would be good to launch at Bloom. His brainwave was to give away two hens free with the coop. He drove to Galway prior to the event to buy hens from his cousin. The hens ended up in our back garden; I was not impressed!

Since, at Bloom, we were always trying to encourage people to visit the showrooms, Henry next came up with the idea of having a Hen Party in Killakee the following Saturday. The lads thought he was joking! But Henry gave out invitations and I think more out of curiosity a good few people said they'd be up next Saturday. When people arrived in the sawmill, Henry would run down to the house to catch the hens for the customers to take away.

We improved the overall look of the stand at Bloom again, encouraging purchases with Bloom Special Offers that were only available at the exhibition. The giftware sold very well, top sellers being hanging baskets and metal garden furniture and planters.

Danielle, Shirley, Ciara and Henry showcasing our Tidy Tims at Bloom.

Ciara made another cut-out board with the Timbertrove branding, which a lot of people took photos of. Ciara and Henry did the artwork, design and printing of the invitations and brochures in-house, while Danielle and I sourced and set up the giftware shop which entailed a serious amount of hard work in the run up to the exhibition, plus the five days and after the event.

The show was a great success. We left with a book full of orders, mainly for the Tidy Tims, bike storage sheds, potting tables, children's playhouses and metal furniture. More people visited the showrooms following the show and placed orders.

Another few bills paid, keeping the wheels turning!

I decided that the café would open on 27 September 2012. Henry wasn't very impressed with the tight deadline but I knew if there wasn't a date set it would go on for months.

A work plan was put together. I had had my vision board for years. I knew exactly what I wanted; it was going to be totally unique, with the interior finished in timber and decorated with a quirky country-style theme. There would be a stove lighting with candles. The Country Store would have unusual affordable gifts. The customers would enjoy the spectacular views overlooking the Dublin mountains and Dublin bay, while enjoying a freshly brewed barista coffee and freshly prepared home-baked food. I argued with Henry to get to do it my way. I was adamant to go with my gut and stick to my vision!

I took Amanda Pratt's advice and bought second-hand equipment and furniture. Eugene, a brother of an ex-employee, did most of the carpentry work. He was a great worker and an extremely nice guy who unfortunately passed away a few years later. We raised a small amount of money through an angel investor to cover the costs of setting up the café.

Danielle and Ciara, who at the time were 20 and 17, agreed to go to Bewley's with me to complete a Barista course. (To be honest, they weren't given a choice).

Our new Café … and the Country Store.

I asked so many people in the industry for advice. Most of them said, "Buy in frozen and don't go to the hassle of baking". But while I knew nothing about running a café at the time, I did know it had to be different. I was conscious customers would pass other cafés along the way to Timbertrove. Frozen food would not be an incentive to visit our café. So even though we weren't baking the food ourselves, I knew it had to be freshly-baked. I sourced scones and cakes from a local bakery, which I collected each morning. I also sold chocolate bars with the coffees and teas.

Through Going for Growth, I met Anne O'Leary, a very successful food industry entrepreneur, who said that if I wanted any advice, she would be glad to help. As I was totally new to the food business and terrified, I took Anne up on her kind offer.

When she arrived at the café, the first thing Anne noticed was the chocolate bars on the counter. She wasn't impressed. I said, "I've just bought them"; she replied, "I don't care. Eat them. Give them away. Just get rid of them. You won't make money selling bars".

When she saw we didn't bake the scones and cakes ourselves, again she said, "You need to bake yourself if you're going to make a profit". She kindly offered to show myself, Danielle and Ciara how to make scones, crumbles, and apple pie. I was so happy to get such valuable advice; the last thing I needed was to lose money!

More advice: "keep it simple"! So we designed the menu around sandwiches, soup and cakes, keeping it traditional, authentic and simple.

Olivia Lane O'Brien, another food industry contact, helped us on the sandwich fillers. Food waste was the key factor in designing the menu. I remember Olivia saying, "This is going to be a goldmine! It's so quirky and unique!"

Ciara designed the café's logo; I had picked colours that sat nicely beside the Timbertrove brand.

We opened on 27 September with very few customers. I was so nervous; I kept looking into the empty café, thinking "This had better work!" I remember Adrian, who was the first employee and now general manager, arriving in that first weekend with his wife Marie and finding the place was empty. When he left, it was still empty and I knew he was thinking "Shirley has blown it this time!"

We opened six days: Tuesday to Sunday. Bernie, my sister-in-law, helped during the week, along with a couple of girls from a Chinese restaurant where we knew the manager. Danielle, Ciara, and their friend Aisling worked the weekends.

We did very little advertising at first, in case we had any teething problems. As time went by, people started to come in; most would have been visiting the sawmill. We did a leaflet drop, advertised locally, and emailed the customers from our database of contacts from the various exhibitions we'd been at. And we were featured in the Small Firms Association's newsletter.

The Halloween and Santa events introduced new customers to the café and showrooms. Quickly, the café became a welcome addition to the business; each day, it got busier and busier. It brought a great

Shirley's contribution to an article, "Weathering the Storm: Changing the Business to Meet the Circumstances".

atmosphere to the place; the carpark was full again, between café and timber customers. The doom and gloom were gone. The staff were happier. The supplier reps couldn't believe the buzz; I was able to bring them in for a coffee and update them on their account and keep them happy.

I now had more time to focus on developing the business, which was increasing sales month by month on both the timber side and café.

During the year, we successfully secured some good contracts: Cosgrave Developments – to manufacture and erect fencing and sheds on one of their sites; the Ritz-Carlton Hotel in Powerscourt – to design, manufacture and erect a playground and chess board outdoors; Alexandra College – to design, manufacture and fit a playground; and OPW – to supply native timber cut to size for a custom bridge.

Timbertrove fencing.

A custom home office.

Despite the setback with the snow for the first quarter of the year, we achieved an increase in sales and further reduced the losses. There was now a little bit of light in the tunnel; sales had stopped falling and losses were almost gone. Onwards and upwards for 2013!

The outdoor chess set installed at the Ritz-Carlton Hotel (now The Powerscourt Hotel), Co. Wicklow.

BETTER TIMES

ON THE UPTURN

Henry and I were looking forward to 2013. We felt quite confident that the worst of the recession was behind us. We were still tight financially; however, the sales had steadily increased month on month the previous year:

- Shed and fencing sales continued to increase, mainly in the domestic market.

- There was a slight increase with the building sites. One builder we had been dealing with for years purchased a substantial amount of the slip-resistant Latitude decking for a site.

- The Tidy Tims continued to sell well, along with the log stores and coal bunkers we had added to our range.

- The café was attracting more people to our premises, which helped with the timber sales and giftware.

With sales increasing, we were determined to make a profit this year; we just couldn't afford to lose any more money. However, we had lost the task teams we had set up and, since the recession, most of the internal systems had gone by the wayside too. We needed to rebuild the business – but in a different way!

In my reading, I came across a book, *The Lean Start-up*, which led me to the Toyota Production System. I was fascinated, because I could relate to it from my time working in the motor trade. The system is based on 14 principles:

1. Base your management decisions on a long-term philosophy, even at the expense of short-term financial goals. The right process will produce the right results.

2. Create continuous process flow to surface problems.

3. Use "pull" systems to avoid over-production.

Henry & Shirley – and lots of panels!

4. Level out the workload (work like the tortoise, not the hare).

5. Build a culture of stopping to fix problems, to get quality right the first time.

6. Standardised tasks are the foundation for continuous improvement and employee empowerment.

7. Use visual control so no problems are hidden.

8. Use only reliable, thoroughly-tested technology that serves your people and processes.

9. Grow leaders who thoroughly understand the work, live the philosophy, and teach it to others.

10. Develop exceptional people and teams who follow your company's philosophy.

11. Respect your extended network of partners and suppliers by challenging them and helping them improve.

12. Go and see for yourself to thoroughly understand the situation.

13. Make decisions slowly by consensus, thoroughly considering all options; implement decisions rapidly.

14. Become a learning organisation through relentless reflection and continuous improvement.

Basically, I took each one of these principles and adapted it into language suitable for our timber business. Later, I produced a document called "The Timbertrove Way" using the principles so that existing and new employees would know how to create a continuous flow throughout the organisation eliminating waste.

When I met Julie Sinnamon, the CEO of Enterprise Ireland, at the Going for Growth conference held in Barberstown Castle, she mentioned an upcoming Enterprise Ireland Lean Management visit to the engine plant at Toyota in Wales. The visit was aimed at director, senior manager and board member women and was planned to support the national effort to enhance the engagement of women within business to drive sustainable competitiveness.

During the workshop with the Toyota team, we were brought out onto the floor to see exactly how the plant was run. It was unbelievable to see the vision boards, so everyone knew what was happening –

particularly as they had a few shifts running every day. If there was an issue between staff, they were brought to a meeting room to iron out the problems and come up with solutions. The room had no table, chairs, or windows. Everyone was visible in their offices, and they even had a training room where new staff had to go through a hands-on programme before they would be recruited.

Prior to the visit, I had read *The Toyota Way: The Toyota Way to Lean Leadership* and also the *Field Book*. I wanted to maximise my visit to the plant. We had dinner with the Toyota team, which was a great opportunity to discuss how I wanted to implement lean practices into both the timber side of our business and the café.

T he CEO of one of our suppliers arrived at the café one day, quite aggressively demanding immediate payment of the remaining balance due to them. After a long lecture on how we should be running our business, he threw a brown envelope on the table serving us with a notice to wind up the company. Fortunately, there were no customers present at the time, but Danielle and Ciara were working in the café and couldn't believe what was happening. They were in tears! But Henry and I were adamant we were not going to let this distract us from the business – although it was a very difficult and stressful situation – so we handed the problem to our solicitor to deal with.

We were summoned to the High Court for Timbertrove to be wound up, on the basis that we had made no effort to pay the account, despite the fact Timbertrove was making the payments as agreed with the supplier's solicitor and had not defaulted on the payment plan.

Henry and I arrived in court with our barrister and solicitor. When the case was called, the other barrister told the judge that we weren't making any effort to pay the account. Our barrister said he had evidence that Timbertrove was making payments as agreed, so the case was adjourned.

The second time, outside the court, their barrister agreed Timbertrove had been making payments and hadn't defaulted. However, he insisted Timbertrove pay their side's legal fees. On this basis, the case was struck out and we continued making the payments as previously agreed; but now three extra payments were added to cover the legal fees.

The whole affair caused Henry and me so much stress, worry and time, together with the expense of hiring a legal team. And no one from the other company even bothered to show up in court!

I was approached by RTÉ to be interviewed by Sean O'Rourke. I was very honoured, and it was obviously great advertising for the company – particularly for the café which was almost a year open. We became a retail destination, open seven days a week – unlike our competitors! One rep we had been dealing with for over 20 years said to me, "Who would have thought a café could turn a sawmill around, with the top selling product now being a scone?"

One Sunday, I was working in the café when a lady arrived in, enquiring if I was looking for a manager. Sheila lived less than five minutes down the road and had previously worked for a café with a similar set-up and menu to ours. I tried to hold back my excitement! I couldn't believe our luck and hired Sheila on the spot as our baker and General Manager. She has a terrific personality, always bubbly and smiling. She is great at managing and everyone loves her! More importantly she is great at baking; her scones are amazing!

A few months later, a landscaper, Sean, who we had been dealing with for years, said to Adrian, "If you are ever looking for someone to work in your café, my wife wants to move from the café she's working in". I interviewed Breda and hired her. Again, she had great experience, a lovely personality and lived locally. She became our Assistant General Manager and made a great team with Sheila. Both are still managing the café. Again baking was no bother to her, she was great!

Sheila and Breda brought the expertise we needed to run the café. They were terrific with the customers, and they had the same banter and *craic* that was instilled in the company over the years. They fitted into my vision perfectly.

We soon started to build up a steady flow of customers, the food and coffee were good, kept simple and authentic! The customers enjoyed the warm welcome and a chat with the girls.

Henry built an office beside the café. It was important for me to see first-hand what was happening. I loved seeing the customers come in; it created such a great buzz after all the doom and gloom we had been through. Most days, I would end up on the till as the girls were too busy on the floor – particularly on Saturdays and Sundays.

As the café grew, so did the paperwork. I ended up splitting my days between the timber side of the business and the café so I could focus either on timber or on food and coffee – two very different businesses!

Timbertrove sheds on display at the Dun Laoire Christmas market.

We received an enquiry to design, manufacture and erect 12 sheds on the seafront in Dun Laoghaire to be used for a Christmas Market. Not alone was it a nice contract, it was great for advertising. We also designed and erected a Christmas crib in the town centre.

As a result of being innovative, looking at things differently and concentrating on the bottom line, we finally achieved a profit this year. Onwards and upwards!

THINK DIFFERENT!

On 24 January 2014, we sent the following letter to all our employees:

As you are aware, over the past few years we have been operating on very tight budgets and resources. We recognise and appreciate that you have all worked with us through these tough times.

One of the problems we were experiencing was lack of customers which I'm sure you will all agree has been overcome due to the opening of the café, which is already showing signs of having a strong impact on sales this year.

It is vital that we are set up and ready to deal with the demand. We have arranged a meeting on Monday, 1 February, which will commence in the cafe at 1.00pm with lunch; it will run until 5.30pm. We need everyone to attend. (It will be paid as a normal day).

At the meeting we want to discuss in detail the procedures we are currently using and how we can improve on them. In advance of the meeting, we would really appreciate your feedback.

If you could write on the attached sheet any ideas, suggestions and concerns you have. If it's tools, etc, that cost money, we will put these into a budget for when money becomes available. You can leave it in Shirley's office in the enclosed envelope by next Thursday and there is no need to put your name to it. If you prefer to do this in groups, that's fine.

We don't want to waste valuable time talking about the past.

We need to **THINK DIFFERENT!**

2014 ONWARDS AND UPWARDS!

Many thanks
Shirley & Henry

From experience, we had found that if meetings were held late in the afternoons, the staff weren't too eager to raise questions as it would delay the meeting and they wanted to get home. So we decided to hold up production for one afternoon to have the meeting, giving ample time to discuss the operations of the business in detail.

It proved to be a very productive and successful afternoon. All the employees engaged in discussing improvements that everyone would benefit from. Some of the topics discussed to achieve a continuous flow throughout the organisation included:

- Sales monthly targets.
- Procedures for quoting jobs and follow-up to turn into a sale.
- Procedures to contact existing and new customers for new business.
- Job costing system to ensure all timber and materials are charged.
- Stock control system.
- Improve the layout of the yard so each department has its timber and materials at hand to eliminate lost time not charged.

My next task was to look at the timeline from the moment the customer gives us an order to when we collect the payment. The objective was to remove non-value-added waste and reduce the timeline.

We entered the SFA National Small Business Awards again and were Finalists in the category "Achievement in Innovation and Excellence in Small Business". A Showcase exhibition was held in Dublin Castle, which was open to the public. This was good advertising for the café and timber products.

Bobby Kerr was very interested in the business and, in his speech, said that he thought opening the café was an ingenious way of turning the business around. He visited the café a few weeks later to carry out an interview with the two of us for his radio show.

We exhibited at Bloom again, which was very successful. At Bloom, RTÉ had relocated to across from our stand, which became a meeting point. We would hear visitors on their phones saying, "We are opposite the Timbertrove stand". The main restaurant and entrance to the show gardens was also close by. Year after year, we were getting better with our display, attracting thousands of people onto our stand.

On the speaking panel at the 2014 Retail Ireland Annual Conference.

I was invited to share our story at the Retail Ireland Mastercard annual conference in the Gibson Hotel with Woodies and Aramark, hosted by Norah Casey. I was not very professional at speaking, unlike the other speakers; however, it was free advertising for the company, and I never like to miss an opportunity – especially when it's free!

On the last working day before Christmas, we received a mobile phone call from someone in the bank saying the bank had sold a pool of loans to an asset management company and that Timbertrove was one of the loans sold. They didn't give any more information, so we didn't really know where we stood with our banking facilities. A few months later, we received a formal written notification from the bank confirming they would no longer be dealing with Timbertrove.

It caused a lot of hassle as we had to notify suppliers, customers, finance companies and Revenue with our new bank details. In the meantime, direct debits that had been set up were being returned by the bank, and if customers paid by credit transfer, we had to try and get that money back from the bank.

Months had passed after the bank had closed our account before the new asset management company contacted us requesting the loan to be paid in full. Over the past few years, Henry and I had several meetings with the bank, trying to get the loan restructured. We were not trying to default on the loan; it just made sense in the current environment to have it restructured.

TIP: Never miss an opportunity to promote your business – especially, if it's free!

Fortunately, Rod, a good friend of ours, recommended a solicitor, Barry, who specialised in loan restructuring. At our initial meeting with him, he made it very clear that he took business very seriously and did not deal with messers! We assured him that we were honourable businesspeople trying to survive a recession and had no intentions of defaulting on the loan or any money we owed. All we needed was time!

Barry set up a meeting for us with the asset management company. In fairness, when we explained our position and the difficulties we were experiencing trying to survive the recession caused through no fault of their own, the asset management people were very understanding. A new agreement was reached with a revised monthly amount to be paid by direct debit. In the meantime, they agreed to give us time to approach the banks to refinance the loan.

I applied to two other banks to refinance the loan. I spent endless days compiling projections, budgets, expected profits, etc – with the banks insisting that all the reports came through our accountants, which cost us more money! It was all very frustrating and a total waste of my time.

The café was going from strength to strength and I had proved Henry wrong! We had achieved a profit inside the 17 months! We had gained a reputation for our home baking and our scones were a huge hit.

Danielle and Ciara continued to work in the café, while attending college, spending a lot of time promoting the café on social media channels.

However, the café and Country Store were built where the events were held, so we could no longer facilitate the Halloween and Santa events. Nonetheless, we achieved sales of over €2m and increased profits. We headed into 2015 with more light in the tunnel!

The signs were evident at Bloom that people were spending money again. We secured a lot more orders at the show and after. We also secured more contracts with builders and there was an increase in the trade accounts. Now that we were back on the building sites, we were using the mini-diggers, dumpers, trucks, and trailers again. Most were badly in need of maintenance as they had been lying up for so long.

Henry had met Philip back in the 1980s and become good friends. They used to go over to the UK together and import trucks, which were a lot cheaper there at the time. Since Philip retired, he started to carry out the odd repair on our trucks and one thing led to another until he was literally looking after the whole fleet.

He was brilliant! He had a hardback book – and still does – in which he recorded every

Philip signwriting the new van.

DOE, NCT, repair or service he carried out on a vehicle. He had a great eye for checking over a vehicle before purchasing. Bear in mind all our trucks were bought second-hand – and most of the machinery too. The lads gave him a terrible time slagging – and still do. He is part of the furniture!

We had finished another successful year!

THE NEXT GENERATION

Danielle graduated from UCD with a Business degree and decided to go to work in San Francisco with her friend Aisling, who was working in the café at the time. Obviously, it would have suited us if Danielle had worked in the business full-time; however, we knew it would be a good experience for her to work for another company and support herself paying rent and utilities. Danielle secured a job in the headquarters of a major American household furniture and décor retailer.

With the timber sales and staff increasing, plus the café, there was a huge increase in the administration and financial work for me. Much and all as we were hoping Danielle would return in a year, we wanted it to be her decision not ours, to avoid any regrets later; so we sat tight.

On her return from San Francisco, Danielle returned to work in the family business, taking on the role of Business Development Manager. Henry and I were delighted, as the workload had increased enormously, especially as the builders' sites became active again.

Within a very short time of her arrival, Danielle established a wonderful rapport with the existing management and employees. She focused on re-introducing the lean management systems compiled in "The Timbertrove Way" manual.

Vincent Langan, the consultant Enterprise Ireland had previously appointed to help us, rejoined the team to work with Danielle. Together, they fostered and promoted a continuous improvement environment throughout the organisation.

It was so good to see an increase in the number of customers visiting the sawmill and spending money again. There was a great atmosphere about the place and the staff were all happy to be busy again.

We were now running two different types of business. While the fundamentals applied to both, there was a lot of other differences between manufacturing timber products and baking. And, as always, there were a few challenges! The car park was very busy trying to accommodate both café customers and timber products customers, as well as landscapers' vans and trailers, along with our own trucks that were all back on the road. And then there were suppliers' trucks delivering timber and materials to the yard, along with trucks delivering to the café.

The timber business was seeing a steady growth in sales; however, the profits were not following suit. We needed to look at the job costing and see which jobs were profitable and which were not. Since the business has so many variables, it is difficult to get a true cost on each job.

Danielle preparing timber samples for customers.

The supply and fitting of fencing and the manufacturing of custom-made products were causing problems. This work was more time-consuming, and it was difficult to get the pricing right. So we decided to focus our attention on improving our standard range of products and eliminating the need for custom-made items.

Danielle has always enjoyed accountancy, so she took a keen interest in watching the figures. Vincent and herself set monthly targets and budgets for the sales, labour, and margins. As Vincent always says, "What gets measured, gets managed"!

Henry, Danielle, Vincent and I met every month to review the month's performance and to make sure we were on track. If there were any issues, we were able to quickly make changes.

In the meantime, Danielle focused on reviewing the job costing. In addition, she took over running the timber side of the business alongside Henry.

I continued looking after the finances, Revenue and bank, while developing and improving the café/takeaway business.

With the success to date, it was obvious the potential was there to grow the café business further. Through Going for Growth, I met Bláthnaid Bergin, a food consultant who owns a company called The Business of Food. I explained that I wanted to learn about kitchen management, stock control and waste. Blathnaid proposed that I attend one of her courses. The course was one day a week for six weeks, in Limerick. Danielle and I both attended the course and found it brilliant, covering exactly what we needed to learn and more.

Literally, from the time Conor could walk, he loved machinery. He was very enterprising and always trying to figure out ways of making money.

Early on, he had a little log business going. I remember collecting him from school: I still don't know how he managed it, but he was always the first one out the gate. He would jump into the car and start texting back his customers who were looking for logs. I never knew how his day went in school, since he hadn't time to talk about it.

At one stage, Conor approached us with a proposal. He had figured out that he would be better off with home schooling because he could do his five days' school in two days and use the other three days to run his business and make money. Henry and I said, "No way!"

Conor at work in his log business.

During the summer one year, he decided to buy and sell topsoil. Henry recalls how he would drive the tractor with Conor on a Saturday morning to a local farmer to get bags of topsoil. Even though Conor was well able to drive, he was still too young to get his licence.

Henry recalls giving out to Conor one Sunday evening, saying, "You never unloaded the topsoil out of the trailer". This meant, on Monday, Henry would have to unload it, costing time and money. On Monday mid-morning, Conor texted Henry from school, saying, "Dad, don't bother unloading the trailer because I have all the topsoil sold".

Conor was so frustrated not being able to drive his John Deere tractor on the road, always having to wait on Henry instead, that he hired one of his friends, Ned, to drive the tractor for him. Conor counted the days to being 16. On his 16th birthday, he applied for his tractor licence and, to no-one's surprise, passed his test first time. There was no looking back!

I did everything to try and get him to study for his Junior Cert. I said, "At least do well in Maths and English, Conor. You will need them to run your business". He replied, "What do you want to know, Mum? I just Google it and I have the answer"! There was no way we could keep him in school any longer, we just had to give in. The school principal and teachers weren't surprised; they well knew what he was like.

Conor's first truck – bought before he even had a driving licence!

Conor was a great networker. When Conor got to know the drivers who had been delivering timber to the yard for years, he knew everything about them. He was great at asking questions and learning from people.

He worked for a few local farmers and became very interested in agricultural contract work. He ended up buying several machines to do the work, including a top-of-the-range baler. Later, he moved into hedge-cutting and construction and agricultural ground works.

Obviously, it would have been great if he had stayed and worked in the sawmill full-time. But, like Danielle, we felt it was better that he went and tried his own thing first and made his own mistakes.

Conor hedgecutting in Kildare.

Conor collecting panels for delivery – under Henry's watchful eye!

In recent years, Conor has become more involved with the Timbertrove business. He has set up an additional manufacturing site for the timber panels, which has helped keep our stock levels fulfilled during the busy season and meet the increasing demand – always a struggle in the past.

He has also more recently taken over Henry's role with the building sites. He is the main point of contact for the fencing contracts, and arranges the pricing, materials, and labour.

Visiting Ciara in Amsterdam.

Ciara graduated from NCAD in 2017 with a degree in Fine Art, Sculpture & Visual Culture, spending a semester through the Erasmus programme at HKU, the University of the Arts, in Utrecht in The Netherlands.

At the NCAD Graduation Show, she was awarded a six-month residency at the Fire Station Artist Studios in Dublin, where she won the Digital Media Graduate Award.

In June 2018, Ciara moved to New York with a Graduate Visa and gained a range of experience:

- Gallery Assistant at the Whitney Museum of American Art.

- Internship in Petzel Gallery.

- Studio Assistant for Shahzia Sikander.

- Studio Assistant for Nancy Lorenz.

In addition, during her time in the US, she spent 10 weeks in Aspen, Colorado, after receiving an Artist in Residence Award from the Anderson Ranch Arts Center.

Ciara on her graduation day.

From New York, Ciara went on to do her Master's in the Dirty Art Department at the Sandberg Instituut, Amsterdam, graduating in June 2022.

Meanwhile, she continued working part-time for the business on our website and marketing material.

We were interviewed by Sean Gallagher and featured in the *Sunday Independent*.

And when Sean published his book, *Secrets to Success*, containing inspiring stories from leading entrepreneurs, compiled from six years of interviews published in the business section of the *Sunday Independent* newspaper, our story featured in it.

The O'Kelly family, celebrating with Sean Gallagher at the launch of his book, Secrets to Success.

We were thrilled to be a Finalist in the South Dublin County Business Awards category "Best place to eat".

We exhibited again at Bloom, with an even better display – we're getting good at this!

The Timbertrove stand at Bloom 2019.

In the café, we had outgrown our small deli cake display. So we extended the prep area and fitted new display counters. That instantly increased sales as, when customers were leaving the café, many would pick up some cakes to take home.

We fitted out a separate area with a second coffee machine for take-away customers. This attracted cyclists and walkers with their dogs, since it suited both groups to sit outside.

However, after three-and-a-half years negotiating and submitting figures, we were told the asset management company was not prepared to continue offering us loan facilities. We explored every possibility – even considering borrowing from moneylenders, but that was way too expensive and would cause us more problems in the long run. But, in 2019, a few days before Christmas, our solicitor concluded a final deal with the asset management company. A very good friend of ours and his partner agreed to give us the financial support to make it happen.

Conor, Ciara, Henry, Shirley and Danielle in the Timbertrove yard.

We have demonstrated the resilience, passion, and determination it takes to run a successful business. We constantly strive to improve and be unique. We have never been afraid of change and adapting. We are always researching and developing, educating ourselves and learning from other successful entrepreneurs around the world. The café has gone from strength to strength, increasing sales and profit each year. Henry got it wrong! The banks got it wrong! Not to mention a lot of other people! My motto is: "listen to advice and go with your gut".

Turnover grew from IR£34,495 in 1986 to €3.9m in 2007, dropped to €1.3m in 2011 and has climbed back to just over €3m (and profitability) in 2019. We have paid every supplier, financial institution and the Revenue in full. We achieved our dreams!

Such a relief! This marked the official end of the recession for Henry and me, finally after 11 years.

So when Oprah Winfrey announced her tour "Oprah's 2020 Vision: Your Life in Focus" for 4 January 2020 in Fort Lauderdale in Florida, with special guest Lady Gaga, I decided to celebrate the end of the recession and treat myself to a trip.

Oprah's 2020 Vision: Your Life in Focus show …

… and the Ford Mustang 5-litre that got me there!

I flew to our house in Florida. Henry had booked a car for me to pick up at the rental company in the airport. But when I realised it was a small standard car, I upgraded it to a Mustang 5-litre convertible. I hit the highway the next morning on a four-hour trip to Fort Lauderdale in the convertible.

The event was sold out with 50,000 people present. Most likely, I was the only Irish girl there!

I came home totally fired up, motivated and feeling very positive for the year ahead. I was convinced it was going to be a wonderful and successful 2020.

I was so wrong!

COVID-19 STRIKES

Henry and I were so excited for 2020 as it was our first year since the recession that we felt we had a clear mindset to focus on developing our business, Timbertrove. No more distraction from debts owed to suppliers, the Revenue or the banks! A clean slate to start the New Year!

But the first case of Covid-19 was diagnosed in Ireland on 1 March 2020. It spread rapidly and, by mid-March, there was talk of the country going into lockdown. Even before St. Patrick's Day, sales had started to decline in the café, which resulted in a lot of waste as everything is baked in-house.

We called a staff meeting to discuss the situation. We explained we were concerned for the health and safety of both staff and customers. We asked everyone whether they wanted to continue working or keep safe and go home to their families. We also explained that we would not be able to pay them, and that they would have to claim Social Welfare which would be €203 per week. To our surprise, the staff all wanted to go home as they were very worried about coming into close contact with Covid-19.

After the horrors of the 2008 recession, Henry and I never imagined that we would be laying off 40 employees again! I was devastated; I never dreamt I would be closing the café. I always thought that, if anything happened again, the café would be safe as people would always be able to afford a scone and coffee!

We were left with a yard full of bales of timber and finished stock and the fridge and deli full of food – and no staff. But, even at this stage, we thought the business would be closed for maybe a week!

Shirley, Ciara and Henry looking at a quiet yard, empty of customers, at the start of lockdown.

The following week, the Government announced the country would go into full lockdown from 27 March for eight weeks. To help businesses, the Government introduced the Temporary Wage Subsidy Scheme, which allowed employers to pay staff 70% of their net wages, with Revenue refunding the company's bank account within 24 hours. This was great for the employees, as it was a significant increase on the €203 from Social Welfare. In addition, business rates were waived for six months, and extensions were given on tax liabilities with the Revenue. This all helped to make a bad situation a little better.

Our experience of the recession helped us to stay positive and focused. We knew our overheads during closure were manageable and we felt that Covid-19 actually had brought a once-in-a-lifetime opportunity. After 35 years in business, Henry and I decided to take time out to revaluate the business and our personal life. We had been through many challenges, setbacks, highs, and lows over the years and managed to survive. It was a real treat to be able to sit as a family and have our meals together, without the distraction of work – something we rarely got to do!

We discussed in detail where the business was at and what we wanted the future to look like. We went through the processes and procedures we were using throughout the business. We looked at what was working and what wasn't. We also looked at the overall layout of the timber yard and manufacturing departments.

From the original hayshed over the years, we had kept adding on bits of sheds and covered space, mostly over the winter months when business was slow. Being open six days a week, it was impossible to carry out any major work. But lockdown now gave Henry and Conor an opportunity to carry out improvements that would increase production and efficiency.

Danielle and Ciara devised a plan to build/improve the website to make it easier for the customer to purchase online. Although we had been trading online over the past couple of years, we never really had time to promote it. This

Danielle working from home during Covid lockdown on the Timbertrove website.

exercise entailed going through every single product and adding more information and photos. They also set up better delivery and payment options. They were continually updating the website with Covid-19 restrictions and responding to emails throughout the closure.

I put my time to good use by re-organising our offices and preparing the café for re-opening.

Danielle, Conor and Ciara working during shutdown.

To comply with the "Return to Work Safety Protocol" issued by the Government and to protect the safety of our staff and customers, we:

- Redesigned the sales office to allow for social distancing.

- Redesigned the showroom layout, to restrict access by the customers.

- Fitted new screens at the customer service counter, and designed and printed safety signs for the appropriate areas.

- Designed and fitted a chute from the sales office to the manufacturing area where the job cards were fed in at the sales office and taken out in the yard.

- Redesigned the car park layout, with collection points for pre-paid orders separate from parking for other customers.

Very little rest for the O'Kelly family during closure!

On 1 May, the Government announced the "Roadmap for Ireland". On 7 May, we posted an update on our website with a banner across the top in red, saying:

Re-opening 18 May
Pre-order Online Now

By midnight on Sunday, 17 May, we were absolutely amazed with the volume of orders placed online – a huge increase on our online sales pre-Covid. It was a great advantage being paid in full and having the timber and finished products in stock for immediate dispatch.

Big changes in the yard.

After the first week, things got even busier – and more challenging. The phones were constantly ringing, along with a constant flow of customers at the sales counter. We were trying to catch up with orders in the system from March – meanwhile, online orders were coming through at a fast rate. We had to quickly redesign our internal processes to deal with the orders and payments.

In preparation for the re-opening of the café, we had to make a lot of changes to comply with the "Return to Work Safety Protocol". When we finally reopened on 27 May 2020, we were starting from scratch! We had thrown out most of the dry ingredients and juices, which had all gone out of date.

I was delighted to see the team back to work. I had really missed them, and the *craic*, and I think they felt the same. It was lovely to hear the customers say how much they missed us and their treats. They were so supportive. From time to time during Covid, customers would ask, "Will ye be OK?" I reassured them all that Timbertrove are fighters!

Soon another lockdown came along, and the indoor seating closed again. But with the travel restrictions, there were a lot of people walking the Hellfire Club and Massy's Wood, which was great for us as we had lost so much revenue with the closure. We had huge queues at the café for take-away coffees, particularly at the weekends and the carpark was crazy.

We quickly adapted by redesigning the take-away area to deal with the demand. We fitted new counters with protective screening and relocated our cash till. We changed the entrance to allow customers to queue outside – with one door in and one door out. We designed a menu board for the outside wall, showing photos of the various food items on offer, so customers could make their choices before entering. It was extremely safe using the 2-metre social distance rule.

Covid-protected: Patrycja, Marie, Shirley, Sheila, Breda and Jenny are ready to greet customers. Fáilte!

A lot of customers complimented us on the new layout. Many preferred to sit outside in the fresh air where they felt safer. Thankfully, we have a large outdoor area with a lovely setting overlooking the Dublin mountains. We increased the seating outside, extended our barn seating area and added heaters. We transformed our timber display sheds into dining sheds – customers loved this as it offers a private and unique setting to enjoy their snack. Henry designed and built outdoor dining pods and a secure bike rack for cyclists.

The café completely shifted from mainly full-service indoor seating, to a take-away business with outdoor seating only. When the Covid restrictions were eventually lifted, we struggled with how we could reopen the indoor seating and still manage the level of efficient service we were providing for our take-away customers.

Lack of space always has been a challenge for us. Before the café existed, Timbertrove had use of the entire premises and still always needed more storage facilities. With the growth of the café, both businesses were squeezed for space. The car park is usually at maximum capacity, made worse by some walkers who leave their cars in our car park for hours while they explore the surrounding areas! Since, due to our location, customers must park on the premises, as there is no street parking. We employed a full-time car park attendant to manage the outdoor area.

After many discussions about layouts and changes, we decided to not reopen the indoor seating. This was not an easy decision – and is still not final.

We know that it's important to adapt and change in business. At the moment, the current arrangement is working well, and we have plans to evolve our take-away business.

I suppose we are victims of our own success! The business has outgrown the car park, which we never imagined would be an issue in the early days!

Other challenges we were faced with included:

- The nationwide shortage of ingredients, which led to price increases on a few occasions.
- Shortages and massive increases in the cost of take-away packaging, such as our branded cups and bags, along with disposable plates and cutlery.
- All the PPE (personal protective equipment) became extremely expensive.
- And that's not to mention the inflation in our utility bills.

The new branded van; the Café's new 10-tray oven; our special scones; and a treat box.

However, there were positives too:

- We extended our kitchen, giving our bakers more space to deal with the increased volumes of cakes sold.

- We upgraded from our two-tray oven to a 10-tray oven, and . from our domestic fridges and freezers to a commercial walk-in fridge/freezer.

- We purchased a second-hand van and had it sign-written for corporate deliveries.

- We introduced new menu options, including a vegan menu, and a pet menu! Our Pupcakes and Puppuccino are now big sellers! We also added more take-home options, including treat boxes, full cakes and sandwich platters.

Danielle and Ciara built a website for the café, which allows online ordering. I am so proud of the success of the Timbertrove Café and Country Store. It has been amazing to watch it grow and grow over the past 10 years. I knew nothing about running a café when I started, so the lesson here is that you can do anything if you put your mind to it. Take advice, go with your gut, and have the passion and determination to succeed!

The advice from Amanda Pratt and Anne O'Leary was right:

Buy secondhand equipment, table and chairs and see what happens! If you want to make money, bake it yourself!

The Timbertrove Café and Country Store's motto is:

Home baked in the heart of the Dublin Mountains!

And I always keep in mind a saying I came across on the WorkingWomen.com website:

One of the best feelings in the world is watching things finally start falling into place after having watched them fall apart for so long.

WE ACHIEVED OUR DREAM!

Our story – the story of Timbertrove – is quite simple: we followed our dream in setting up and running a successful business, while achieving our goals along the way.

We have walked the talk! We built the business from the ground up with very little money, just a dream! We fought through the insurance crisis and a global recession – and we rebuilt the business. When we were struck with Covid-19, we took the opportunity during lockdown to re-evaluate the business and come back stronger.

We are proud of the reputation Timbertrove has gained over the past 35 years for top quality products and service. I am extremely proud of the success of the Timbertrove Country Store and Cafe. It has been amazing to watch it grow from the secondhand equipment and furniture, the small kitchen and deli to what it has become 10 years later. We are well known for our freshly home-baked cakes and sandwiches in the heart of the Dublin mountains.

Henry and I are delighted to see Danielle, Ciara and Conor all doing so well for themselves. We're immensely grateful to them for all their hard work in the business over the years – time sacrificed from their friends and other activities – from when they were small children onwards! I'm especially grateful to the two girls for their 'volunteering' when I was in throes of setting up the café and so reliant on them.

We are so thankful to our dedicated team who stuck with us through thick and thin. They go above and beyond to welcome our customers. They are very much a part of the success of the business – we wouldn't still be standing without them

Special thanks are due to our customers, who have supported our business. I have noticed – particularly since Covid – that more people want to support their small local business, which is so important. It's very tough on some small businesses trying to compete against the multinational companies.

We are not millionaires, nor did we plan to be! We are comfortable; it was never our intention to become a multinational business.

Over the past 35 years, we have learnt – often the hard way – what it takes to run your own successful business. The key elements are:

- Passion, determination, resilience and working smart.
- Being innovative and adaptable.
- Continuous improvement: as the business grows, so will its needs. Manage and embrace change.
- Never be afraid to take advice – and then go with your gut.
- Build a good team around you; hire people who have the skills you don't. Give them authority. Be honest. Trust and respect your employees.

- Work on the business, not in the business. Don't be a busy fool.
- Build good relationships with your suppliers and customers. Provide top quality products and service. Don't take shortcuts.
- Constant learning, through reading and listening from other successful entrepreneurs.
- Networking: surround yourself with great people who experience similar setbacks and challenges.
- Look after your health and wellbeing; it's a very important asset to the business!
- When things get tough (which they will), stay positive, look for the opportunities and remind yourself why you started the business in the first place.
- Be prepared to fight for your business. Had we not fought the insurance crisis, the supplier who wanted to wind up the business or the global recession, Timbertrove would not be here today!

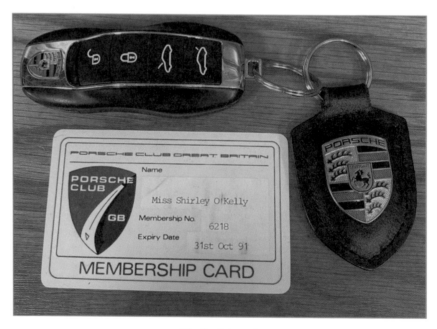

The final dream!

From our experience, the most valuable piece of advice is to know your numbers. We have monthly meetings – normally around the 12th of the month – with myself, Henry, Danielle and Conor (when we can get him off a site!).

I produce the profit and loss account (with a separate set of accounts for the café/takeaway business), showing the total sales, purchases, overheads and the gross margin and profit or loss for the month. Danielle produces her spreadsheet with sales, labour percentage and stock figures *versus* budget, so we can measure productivity. We then go through the debtors and creditors listings, along with an update on the cashflow.

I can't emphasis enough how important it is to **do this every month**. If anything is going wrong, you can see it immediately and act quickly! What gets measured gets managed!

While it is important to delegate, you as the owner need to be in control of your finances. **After all, it's your money and no one else will treat it the same as you!** Unless you're fortunate enough to have a trusted partnership like myself and Henry!

Depending on your business, other things you need to do include:

- Have a computer system suitable for your business. In our case, we have a Sage accounting and point of sale system along with Clover point of sale for the takeaway. Danielle has designed various spreadsheets to produce the additional figures we need to measure.

- Do your research. Who is your market, who are you going to sell your product to and how much will they pay for it? How much will it cost you to produce it, and how much do you need to charge for it after you have taken your overheads and profit into account?

- Invest wisely in marketing and brand-building.

- Install Lean systems, like the Toyota Production System.

- Set up and use purchasing control and stock control systems.

- Have a reliable accountancy/tax adviser firm and solicitor.

- Keep your debtors and creditors within agreed credit terms.

- Stay up to date with Revenue.

- Update your cashflow spreadsheet daily.
- Get into a position where you are not totally reliant on your bank, especially when things get tough!
- Have a rainy-day bank account.

I'd also recommend being a member of the Small Firms Association, whose parent organization is IBEC. SFA is the voice of small business in Ireland. It runs great networking events, through which we have met numerous people over the years who have become clients, suppliers or advisors. And, as you've seen from our story, we have received tremendous exposure and recognition for our business through the National Small Business Awards, all for free!

Being a member of Going for Growth for women entrepreneurs is a fantastic opportunity to meet and learn from their experienced Lead Entrepreneurs. It's very comforting to be able to share your story and issues with likeminded women in a confidential environment.

And, if you are in the food industry, I recommend "The Business of Food" run by Bláthnaid Bergin, Restaurant Advisor.

Our current management structure is :

- **Henry:** responsible for the timber side of the business.
- **Shirley:** responsible for the finances of the timber business, along with the Country Store and Café.
- **Danielle:** Business Development Manager and responsible for the day-to-day operations on both sides of the business. Her focus is measuring sales *versus* labour costs, as well as managing production, stock control and waste.
- **Conor:** managing the fencing on sites with the builders.
- **Ciara:** works part time on our marketing and creative tasks.
- **Adrian:** General Manager of Timbertrove for the past 34 years.
- **Sheila:** General Manager of Timbertrove Café for the past 9 years.
- **Breda:** Assistant GM of Timbertrove Café for the past 9 years.

I remember the day a friend/customer was in the café and asked me what Henry's involvement was in the cafe. I replied, "He is our only non-paying customer!"

Dreams without goals are just dreams. I love business. I love socialising with other likeminded businesspeople. I Iove a challenge. I strive on setting and achieving goals. I constantly set targets for myself, particularly when I set up the café. When I smash one goal, I move to the next!

But, without Henry, I wouldn't have had a story to tell. He is – and has always been – my Rock!

RECOMMENDED READING

From my reading over the years, I'd recommend the following books:

- *Awaken Your Power Within* / Gerry Hussey.
- *Flourishing* / Maureen Gaffney.
- *Oversubscribed* / Daniel Priestley.
- *Positivity: Confidence, Resilience, Motivation* / Paul McKenna.
- *Secrets to Success* / Sean Gallagher.
- *Steve Jobs: The Man Who Thought Different* / Karen Blumenthal.
- *The 4 Hour Work Week* / Timothy Ferriss.
- *The 4 Disciplines of Execution* / Chris McChesney, Sean Covey, Jim Huling.
- *The 7 Habits of Highly Effective People* / Stephen R. Covey.
- *The Compound Effect* / Darren Hardy.
- *The E-Myth* / Michael E. Gerber.
- *The Lean Startup* / Eric Ries.
- *Think and Grow Rich* / Napoleon Hill.